NEVER TO LEAVE US ALONE

"Lewis Baldwin, the foremost chronicler of Martin Luther King Jr., traces his prayer life and its huge, enabling force in the fight for human rights. A wonderful book! Read it, and you will be inspired."

David Buttrick
Buffington Professor of Homiletics and Liturgics Emeritus
Vanderbilt University Divinity School

"Lewis Baldwin is one of our most valuable interpreters of the life and thought of Martin Luther King Jr. Out of his sustained engagement with King comes this unforgettable portrait of the theologian, prophet, and American reformer at prayer. It is a necessary and long overdue completion of a portrait and one that will be cherished for years to come."

Richard Lischer
Duke Divinity School
Author of *The Preacher King: Martin Luther King Jr.*
and the Word that Moved America

"This intense probing of the prayer life of Martin Luther King Jr. by Lewis Baldwin brings depth and clarity to the concept of 'praying without ceasing.' In the tradition of an African griot, Baldwin unfolds the story of Dr. King, spirit-filled servant of God, who utilized the power of persistent prayer, plus a constant study of human inequities in an alien land and the search for truth, as all encompassing in the process of 'witnessing for the Lord.' This is not simply another collection of facts about the celebrated 'peaceful warrior.' It is a newly opened window into the heart and soul of a servant-preacher who continues to teach through his understanding and experience of the power of prayer. It should be required of all theological seminarians!"

Melva Costen
Helmar Emil Nielsen Professor Emerita of Worship and Music
Interdenominational Theological Center, Atlanta, Georgia

Martin Luther King at silent prayer in the pulpit; early 1960s.
Photographer: Frank Dandridge.

NEVER
TO
LEAVE
US
ALONE

THE PRAYER LIFE OF
MARTIN LUTHER KING JR.

LEWIS V. BALDWIN

FORTRESS PRESS
MINNEAPOLIS

For my father,
The Reverend L. V. Baldwin,
whose tombstone reads, "He Prayed,"
and for those who seek
the spiritual energy that comes through prayer
but are afraid to open themselves
to its
marvelous possibilities

NEVER TO LEAVE US ALONE
The Prayer Life of Martin Luther King Jr.

Scripture quotations from the New Revised Standard Version of the Bible are copyright © 1989 by the Division of Christian Education of the National Council of Churches of Christ in the United States of America and are used by permission.

Cover image © Flip Schulke / CORBIS
Cover design: Laurie Ingram
Book design: Christy J. P. Barker

Library of Congress Cataloging-in-Publication data

Baldwin, Lewis V., 1949–
 Never to leave us alone : the prayer life of Martin Luther King, Jr. / by Lewis V. Baldwin.
  p. cm.
 Includes bibliographical references and index.
 ISBN 978-0-8006-9744-0 (alk. paper)
 1. King, Martin Luther, Jr., 1929–1968—Religion. 2. Baptists—United States—Clergy—Biography. I. Title.
 E185.97.K5B349 2010
 323.092—dc22
 [B]

                    2010015016

The paper used in this publication meets the minimum requirements for American National Standard for Information Sciences—Permanence of Paper for Printed Library Materials, ANSI Z329.48–1984.

Manufactured in the U.S.A.
14   13   12   11   10   1   2   3   4   5   6   7   8   9   10

CONTENTS

FOREWORD

Once again, Lewis V. Baldwin has corrected grievous errors committed by other chroniclers of Martin Luther King Jr. His earlier volumes have corrected the flaws of King "experts" who often overlook or ignore the critical aspects of King's cultural development as an African American and the influence of that development from King's home environment and family at Ebenezer Baptist Church in Atlanta, Georgia. In *There Is a Balm in Gilead*, Baldwin laid the foundation for aspects of King's construct in his person and mission in erasing segregation from the United States and in pointing the nation toward a postracial era. He clearly presented the critical factors that made King who he was, thereby correcting the flaws of other King chroniclers to date.

In this work, Baldwin's novel approach is to examine the prayer life of Dr. King. I do not know if Baldwin had access to Dr. King's self-imposed "Day of Silence," in which he abstained from the distractions of daily life, including the telephone, television, and radio. That day was spent in prayer and meditation and in developing a rigorous discipline of "think time," which he devoted to mapping strategies for the nonviolent campaigns he led. It was this discipline, I believe, that gave King the spiritual and moral strength to withstand the tremendous pressures associated with the forms of resistance, including the possibility and eventuality of his own death by murder. He often said to us, "I won't make forty." He had no martyr complex, but he knew how deeply embedded racism was in the body politic of the nation.

Generations from now, when writing about King has ceased, Baldwin's work about the man and his mission will remain the most definitive. No one living or dead has discovered the "mother lode" as has Baldwin. In this work, Baldwin discovers the mystique of Martin Luther King Jr., and he carefully examines the key to King's strength of spirit against seemingly impossible odds. Establishing justice in an unjust nation was more than a daunting challenge. Baldwin's work, for generations to come, will help us better understand how King accomplished this through prayer and hard work and with the considerable help of the almighty God, in whom King trusted and believed. King's prayer life patently revealed this, and Baldwin has revealed it to us.

Wyatt Tee Walker
Former Chief of Staff to Martin Luther King Jr.
Chester, Virginia

PREFACE

Never to Leave Us Alone was inspired by a keen awareness that no
other book-length work examines the prayers and prayer life of
Martin Luther King Jr. While numerous studies of King's sermons,
speeches, and pulpit style have appeared in published form over the
last half century, his prayers, attitude toward prayer, and practice
of the art and discipline of prayer have been woefully neglected.
This little volume is designed to correct this glaring omission,
while also demonstrating how King's prayer life and reflections on
prayer offer infinite possibilities for the cultivation of positive and
core human values.

The decision to write and publish *Never to Leave Us Alone*
came after repeated but unsuccessful attempts to obtain permission to edit and publish a collection of King's personal prayers,
under the title *Never Alone: The Prayers of Martin Luther King Jr.*
The research for *Never Alone* actually began more than two decades
ago, and the work was completed in 2007. Some seventy-eight
prayers of King were discovered through a careful reading of his
sermons, speeches, and published and unpublished writings, and
I organized them into four categories; namely, Prayers from Student Days, 1948–54; Pastoral Prayers, 1954–68; Sermonic Prayers,
1954–68; and Movement Prayers, 1955–68. The project was made
known to both the King Estate and the Senior Editor of the King

Papers Project at Stanford University in March, 2008, and weeks later I was informed that they had something similar in mind, and that this might create a competitive conflict with projects that the King Estate was pursuing. I also learned later that permissions to publish anthologies or collections could not be granted at that time, especially since various parties were involved in larger discussions of these rights for the King Estate. In any case, I remain hopeful that *Never Alone* will be published in the future and that it will serve as a companion volume to *Never to Leave Us Alone*.

Although the full range of King documents is compulsory reading for anyone interested in his spirituality, his sermons constitute the richest sources for exploring his prayer life. Here one finds not only the civil rights leader's personal prayers but also his favorite prayer lines from scripture and the Christian tradition. These prayer sources, some of which consist of one or two sentences, blend adoration, confession, entreaty, and thanksgiving with meditation, mystery, and wonder. They reveal how King turned to prayer as the foundation of his personal spiritual life, the center of his devotional practice, and a powerful, sacred force in his struggle to liberate and empower people. This material also indicates how King developed prayer as living, passionate speech, sermonic discourse, and pastoral conversation.

I hope that *Never to Leave Us Alone* is a groundbreaking effort to analyze King's prayer life and conception of prayer. King was arguably the most advertised religious figure in America in the 1960s, and his prayer life, philosophy of prayer, and practice of praying are immensely important for understanding him as both a person of faith and a social activist. This study shows that King never reduced prayer to simply inspired speech, religiously informed rhetoric, sacred or soul language, or indulgence in the torrents of passionate oratory. Instead, prayer for King was a gift from God that has infinite dimensions for exploration, a spiritual quality that must be continuously cultivated. It was about facilitating an intimate relationship with the living spirit and leading people into the presence of the Supreme Personality. Thus, *praying time* for King was *sacred time* and *self-purification time*, and prayer became a built-in, structured aspect of his private and public life. King had an all-pervasive sense of the divine presence and of the life-filling richness of prayer, and he consistently noted that praying is about responding in a spirit of humility to the activity of God's grace in daily life.

In a more general sense, this volume explains what King shared about the salient features of prayer and how he refused to separate prayer from his larger effort to craft theologically sound and effective ministries for the church and in the streets. It reveals that King majored in the traditional trajectories of Christian prayer—adoration, confession and supplication, petition, thanksgiving, intercession, meditation, and contemplation—all of which were often combined whenever he recited psalms of prayer, prayers of illumination, communion prayers, hymns of prayer, benedictions, and doxologies in congregational contexts. In King's estimation, all of these devotional forms constituted salient features of the well-defined prayer life, and they were uppermost in his thinking whenever he theologized about prayer and praying. Clearly, there is a need to rethink questions not only about King's theology but also his politics and ethics in light of his prayer life and attitude toward praying.

This book is equally significant for what it reveals concerning King's assault on age-old myths and misconceptions concerning prayer and the art of praying. King rejected the claims, made essentially by atheists, that prayer is a mindless activity, that it speaks to the absence of intellect, and that it is an exercise in futility. For King, prayer involved both head and heart, and praying was designed to stimulate spiritual growth and to inform the mind. King spoke of prayer and the search for the living God in language that penetrated the thinking of people. Furthermore, King was an unwavering critic of the claim that prayer is unproductive and of the Aristotelian notion that God is unmoved by the struggles, cries, and joys of the world. *Never to Leave Us Alone* proves that King modeled a more hope-filled approach to prayer and praying and that he consistently spoke to the efficacy of prayer despite the ambiguities of life in the universe. Consequently, he ignited deep and productive thinking about the task, habit, and possibilities of prayer.

The ways in which King engaged in prayer and praying as creative energy may be the most distinctive angle developed in this work. In King's case, prayer, voiced and unvoiced, became a call to mission or to action. He was convinced that prayer worked as an empowering and liberating force in the context of struggle. He had little patience with those who turned to prayer as a substitute for human initiative or who prayed while ignoring the social maladies that afflict society. A part of his rallying cry was that activism prefaced by prayer can be most effective. This is why King concentrated on persuasive prayer, or prayers of persuasion—the kind that incited listeners to action. In King's civil rights campaigns, prayer became a form of creative energy, a unique spiritual force in which religion, art, and protest coexisted and found vital expression.

King's utilization of prayer as creative energy in his own personal life is not ignored in this volume. In other words, *Never to Leave Us Alone* is not merely about those times when King was lost in the high frenzy of public prayer. It is also about those moments of sacred stillness, of solitude and private prayer, when King found the courage to follow God's will and not his own. It is about the personal spiritual journey behind King's prayer life. Moreover, it highlights King's ability to rise above the doubts and fears that haunted him and to subvert nagging concerns about his own safety in favor of an ethic of risk, sacrifice, and redemptive suffering. In other words, King always found new wisdom and guidance in prayer. Evidently, King's emphasis on private prayer as creative energy was, as the content of this work shows, consistent with his tendency to place spiritual transformation at the center of every action he took as a crusader for freedom, justice, and human dignity. Thus, he was able to confront the relentless pressure of the forces of evil and retrogression without faltering.

Although much is said in this book about prayer as the central element of the weekly rhythm of King's activities as a preacher, pastor, and social activist, the extent to which he reclaimed prayer as both a living tradition and lived theology is no less important. *Never to Leave Us Alone* explains how King's prayer life was enriched with insights and wisdom from a range of experiential, cultural, and intellectual traditions or sources. King reflected the influence of these traditions and sources each time he knelt or bowed in prayer, though he never consciously provided a prayer model or primer on prayer. Because King was functioning in the broad context of Christian traditions, he was always mindful of the transformative power, curative purposes, and therapeutic value of prayer and praying, especially for black people, whose response to oppression had always been largely liturgical. King reclaimed prayer as eloquent, sacred speech, as soulful communication with the God of the universe, and as "a balm" in the quest for healing and deliverance, and this is part of that unique quality that made him such a profound communicator of the Christian faith.

Never to Leave Us Alone concludes that King remains a model of spirituality and godly devotion in these perilous times of globalization, polarization, social regression, and growing cultural cynicism. It is just the beginning of what I hope will be a deeper and more meaningful conversation about how King perceived and employed the art and discipline of prayer in his personal life, the church, and the larger world of civil and human rights struggles, and about the degree to which King's prayer life and philosophy of prayer remain helpful and instructive for us today. If this work reignites intense and positive exchanges about the meaning, task, and possibilities of prayer at all levels of human life and activity, my greatest hope for it will be realized. So let the conversation begin.

ACKNOWLEDGMENTS

I am heavily indebted to several persons for assistance in the conception and writing of *Never to Leave Us Alone*. I was first inspired by a conversation I had more than two decades ago with Lawrence N. Jones of the Howard University School of Religion. While interviewing Jones as part of my research on the cultural roots and legacy of Martin Luther King Jr., this leading voice in black church studies suggested that some focus on the civil rights leader's prayer life would constitute an original contribution to King scholarship. I took the idea to heart and began a search for King's prayers in his published and unpublished sermons, speeches, and writings.

Driven largely by the encouragement that came from Professor Jones years earlier, I completed the first edited collection of King's prayers in 2006. I chose as the title for the volume *Never Alone: The Prayers of Martin Luther King Jr.*, and a contract was finalized with Fortress Press, but the King Estate did not grant permission to publish the work, despite my decision to donate all proceeds to the King Memorial in Washington, D.C. At the urging of colleagues here at Vanderbilt, and especially Drs. Victor Anderson and Herbert Marbury, I then decided to write my own book on King's prayer life, using my previous work as a foundation on which to build. *Never to Leave Us Alone* is the culmination of this effort, and it is a testimony to the lingering influence of Jones, Anderson, and Marbury.

I owe a debt of gratitude to Clayborne Carson, the senior editor of the Martin Luther King Jr. Papers Project at Stanford University. Since 1992, Carson and his staff have published six of an anticipated fourteen-volume edition of King's sermons, speeches, writings, and correspondence, sources that made many of the civil rights leader's prayers accessible to me. These sources helped make *Never to Leave Us Alone* possible. After receiving my completed manuscript collection of King's personal prayers in March, 2008, Carson also agreed to give it a careful reading.

My deepest appreciation is extended to Elaine Summers Rich, an elderly white woman I met in January, 2007, after delivering the annual Martin Luther King Jr. Lecture at Bluffton University in Ohio. During our brief conversation, Elaine told me of a brief encounter she had with King in the 1960s. "I had the feeling that as we spoke," she recounted, "he was actually praying for me." This is the impression Elaine got as she stared into King's eyes. I have not forgotten what she shared with me, and I left her determined to include her story in my book on King's prayer life. Frankly, Elaine rekindled my thinking about the possible impact that a book like this could have on people of different backgrounds even today.

Many thanks to the Reverend Dr. Wyatt Tee Walker, former chief of staff to Martin Luther King Jr., for his many contributions to this work. Despite being ill and largely incapacitated, Walker was a constant source of inspiration and support, and he corrected what would have been serious flaws in my approach and analysis. I was always uplifted and rejuvenated by the letters he wrote me and by our periodic telephone conversations. Walker's decision to write the foreword to *Never to Leave Us Alone* is a great honor to me personally.

I am highly grateful to the staff of both the Martin Luther King Jr. Center for Nonviolent Social Change, in Atlanta, and the Mugar Memorial Library at Boston University for their assistance in locating hundreds of King documents. Cynthia Lewis and Elaine Hall at the King Center were especially helpful in my research. They have always been kind and gracious.

I wish to thank my editors Michael West and Gloria Bengtson for their abiding interest in and support of this project. They stood patiently with me in my frustrating and unsuccessful efforts to secure permission to edit and publish a collection of King's prayers, and *Never to Leave Us Alone* testifies to their devotion to King scholarship. I was thrilled when Michael indicated that Fortress Press would also consider this book for publication.

Michele Rubin of Intellectual Properties in New York deserves much praise for her advocacy on behalf of my work. She tried more than anyone else to obtain permission for the publication of *Never Alone*, my collection of King's personal prayers, and this piece grew largely out of her suggestion that I consider doing a different kind of work on King's spirituality.

I acknowledge with pleasure the contribution of my wife, Jacqueline, who insisted that I not surrender in my determination to do a book on King's art and practice of prayer. Over the more than two decades of my research and scholarship on King, she has been a source of unwavering support and inspiration.

I am eternally indebted to my late parents, the Reverend L. V. and Flora Bell Baldwin, for teaching me how to pray when I was still too young to grasp its full significance. They did not hesitate to resort to the most stringent discipline, including the belt, to make sure that my siblings and I participated in early Sunday morning prayers as a family. Memories of these prayer meetings have not left me, and they account for any special insight I may have brought to this analysis of King's prayers and prayer life.

I owe a lot to those great but unsung voices of prayer to which I was exposed as a child in the churches of rural Alabama: Mr. Beno McNeil, who was known to "ring up heaven," and my own uncle, John Henry Baldwin, who prayed, as we used to say, "with power from on high," and who believed and often said that "prayer changes things." These and other great souls, who now sleep in the great beyond, taught me a lot about the power and the pulsing rhythms of prayer, and I am indebted to them for many of the insights I bring to my analysis of King's experiences of prayer.

Finally, I offer a word of praise and thanksgiving to the God of history, for sustaining me in this very serious and exciting undertaking. I am even more convinced that prayer is an enormously powerful force, which often yields what might otherwise appear impossible or unattainable to the human imagination.

He promised never to leave me, never to leave me alone.

Martin Luther King Jr.

27 August 1967

Martin Luther King at prayer over dinner with his family.
Source: William Diehl, courtesy of Virginia Gunn.

INTRODUCTION

This book is different from every other book about Marin Luther King Jr. In tracing the evolution of King's prayer life, from his childhood in Atlanta, Georgia, to his rise as the most famous and celebrated civil rights leader in American history, this book is critical to our understanding of *how* and *why* King became what Gardner C. Taylor calls "the most authentic spiritual genius in this land."[1] It explains how King combined a deep personal piety with intellectual ability and a profound social vision, and it also helps us to better understand the mystical dimensions of this extraordinary figure.

King said as much about the meaning, significance, and necessity of prayer as any other religious figure in his time, and references to praying regularly appear throughout his sermons, speeches, interviews, and writings. He defined prayer as the human "response to God,"[2] characterizing it as the heart and soul of the Judeo-Christian tradition. He often appealed to the biblical roots of prayer as an authority and guide in his own life and experience of prayer. Some of King's favorite prayer lines came from the psalmist and the Hebrew prophets, who, in his thinking, embodied the biblical ideal of prayer. He delighted in quoting Psalm 139:7-12, which begins with the psalmist's question to God: "Where can I go from Your Spirit? Where can I flee from Your presence?" For King, this passage spoke of God's universal presence and reminded the person who prays that the face of God is never absent.[3] King was also known to quote Isaiah 45:15, in which the prophet blends confession, adoration, and wonder, declaring that, "Truly you are God, who hides Yourself, O God of Israel, the Savior." And there was Habakkuk 1:2, in which King pictured the prophet complaining about Jehovah's silence in the midst of his prayer for help: "Oh Lord, how long shall I cry, and You will not hear!"[4] The civil rights leader apparently had a biblically informed conception of prayer, and he found in these and other Hebrew Bible sources insights into the essence of prayer and support for his view of prayer as a daily conversation and walk with God.

Equally important for King were prayer lines from the New Testament, which appear more frequently in his sermonic discourse. The prayer of the publican or tax collector in Luke 18:13—"God be merciful to me a sinner"—filters through some of King's messages on the nature of the human condition and on the need to keep the "soul open to God."[5] In Luke 22:42, Jesus' cry in the Garden of Gethsemane—"Father, if Thou be willing, let this cup pass from me; nevertheless not my will, but Thine be done"—became King's own prayer, and so did Jesus' sublime utterance from the cross as recorded in Luke 23:34: "Father, forgive them, for they do not know what they do." The same might be said of Jesus' prayer amid "the agony and darkness of the cross" in Matthew 27:46: "My God, My God, why have You forsaken Me?"[6] All of these prayer lines underscored for King the nature of the human condition, the power of love, and the bitter suffering that awaits those determined to transform and redeem society.[7] Jesus' prayers and statements concerning prayer touched King's heart and mind in profound ways while also providing a blueprint for the ideal prayer life. The Lord's Prayer as recorded in Matthew 6:9-13, the prayer that Jesus taught his disciples, was the one King recited most frequently from the New Testament.[8] When it came to the content, discipline, and activity of prayer, Jesus became perhaps more paradigmatic for King than any other biblical, spiritual, and historical example.

But King found other great models of prayer in the history and traditions of the Christian church, beginning with the church fathers. From the *Confessions* of St. Augustine (354–430), the most influential of the fathers of the Western church, King quoted: "Thou awakest us to delight in Thy praise; for Thou madest us for Thyself, and our heart is restless, until it repose in Thee." King also noted that there is something in the yearning spirit that "causes us to cry out with Saint Augustine," "Lord, make me pure but not yet." In King's estimation, St. Augustine acknowledged humanity's utter dependence upon God, captured the emptiness and meaninglessness of the prayerless life, and spoke emphatically to the need for humans to "shake the lethargy from our souls."[9] The following prayer from Francis of Assisi (1182–1226), the thirteenth-century saint and founder of the Franciscan Order, also figured prominently among King's favorite spiritual resources:

> Lord, make me an instrument of Thy peace;
> Where there is hatred, let me sow love;
> where there is injury, pardon;
> where there is doubt, faith;
> where there is despair, hope;
> where there is darkness, light;
> and where there is sadness, joy.

> O Divine Master, grant that I may
> not so much seek to be consoled, as to console;
> to be understood, as to understand;
> to be loved, as to love;
> for it is in giving that we receive;
> it is in pardoning that we are pardoned;
> and it is in dying that we are born to eternal life.[10]

This prayer gave expression to King's core spiritual and social values and affirmed his conviction that genuine self-realization and fulfillment comes through both reverent petitions to God and unselfish action in the interest of the common good. Prayers offered by the Protestant Reformer Martin Luther (1483–1546),

the English Puritan preacher John Bunyan (1628–1688), and the
Methodist founder John Wesley (1703–1791), carried similar
meanings for King; and they, as much as any other sources of spirituality, echoed his belief that the person of faith must always act
on the basis of conscience.[11] In the following, well-chosen quota-
tion from the prayers of the Methodist revivalist George White-
field (1714–1770), King found support for his ecumenical vision,
especially his view that Christian outreach at its best is cooperative
in nature: "God help us, God help us all, to forget party names,
and to become Christians indeed, and in truth."[12] King brought
these prayer sources together in his consciousness with theolo-
gians in his own time, such as Karl Barth, Paul Tillich, Reinhold
Niebuhr, Howard Thurman, and others, thus showing his indebtedness to that broader heritage of the Christian church for much
of his understanding and practice of prayer. Needless to say, King's
own prayers and prayer life became and remain a distinctive and
enduring contribution to that rich spiritual heritage.

But King's sense of the importance and "power of persistent
prayer"[13] extended beyond its central place in the so-called Judeo-
Christian tradition. Evidently, he had other reasons for highlighting prayer as a primary, indispensable, and all-engaging force in the
world, as "one of the elemental functions of human life," and as a reli-
able path in the search for truth and the complete life.[14] As King studied the vast landscape of human history, he saw that the vitality and
efficacy of prayer in personal devotional life had been demonstrated
continuously in the experiences of men and women everywhere. He
also saw that all of the world's great religions shared a devotion to the
practical, spiritual, and ritualistic dimensions of prayer, that prayer
was a unifying element among peoples of different faith traditions.[15]
Moreover, King understood that prayer has a unique role in any serious and legitimate effort to achieve social transformation.

King's prayer life and attitude toward prayer deserve special
attention for several reasons. First, it is a critical and curiously
neglected side of King's life and ministry, let alone of his theology
and ethics. Even King scholars have said little or nothing about the

place of prayer in King's life and thought. This pattern of omission in King scholarship must be corrected if we are to more fully grasp King's spiritual magnitude and theological and ethical fortitude.[16] Second, a study of this nature is necessary for the fascinating lens it affords into King's personal spiritual life. King never separated intellectual ability, moral responsibility, and social praxis from deep personal spirituality and piety. In other words, King realized that the resources of mind, heart, soul, and spirit came together as a necessary precondition for vibrant and successful ministry and mission. Prayer, as he viewed it, was an essential ingredient in this equation.

Third, there is a certain beauty and dynamism in King's practice of and experiences with prayer. He crafted and recited some of the most strikingly and profoundly moving prayers in all of sacred literature.[17] One is immediately struck by the exquisite beauty, eloquence, poetry, and florid prose of those prayers, and how prayer became one of his most effective ways of witnessing, pastorally and prophetically.

Finally, King's conception and practice of prayer are meaningful for persons of faith in contemporary society and the world. His experiences with prayer, theoretically and practically, are informative, instructive, and inspirational, and they invite readers in all ages to a journey of self-exploration, self-analysis, self-surrendering, and self-discovery. Put another way, King's prayer life constitutes one angle from which we might look anew at what he means for our own troubled times.

This study of King's prayer life consists of six chapters. Chapter 1 discusses King in relation to what Harold A. Carter calls "the prayer tradition of black people."[18] In it I conclude that for King the imperative to pray came not only from a sense of his own personal finitude before God but also from a deep consciousness grounded in the African American religious experience, especially the traditions of the black church. Although King challenged and rejected some elements of folk religion such as its rigid biblical fundamentalism and hypermoralism, he retained its strong belief in and practice of praying. This is perhaps the most sweeping conclusion in this chapter. As it further reveals, King fully embodied the genius and power of the black prayer tradition, and what he thought, said, and wrote about prayer are as significant for locating him in that tradition as his own personal prayer life.[19] The substance of this first chapter goes far beyond what is provided in the works of Harold Carter,[20] James M. Washington,[21] O. Richard Bowyer et al.,[22] and the Schomburg Center for Research in Black Culture,[23] all of which explore certain aspects of the African American prayer tradition. Although these sources, with the exception of Carter's groundbreaking piece, offer virtually nothing on King's place in and indebtedness to that tradition, they nevertheless proved beneficial to the development of the conceptual and/or theoretical framework of *Never to Leave Us Alone*.

Chapter 2 traces the development of King's prayer life and thoughts on prayer during his years as a college (1944–48), seminary (1948–51), and graduate student (1951–54).[24] As the chapter indicates, King was searching during these years for a deeper and more authentic spirituality. Serious attention to these formative stages in King's personal, spiritual, and theological odyssey inevitably leads to a range of questions: What spiritual path did King take in those early years, and how did prayer figure into his spiritual quest? What was his definition of prayer? What forms of prayer did he recite, and in what particular contexts did he offer them? To what extent did he embrace prayer as a personal vocation, and how did he go about the task of praying? Did he develop what might be described as *a theology of prayer*? In this second chapter, I offer answers to these and other questions.[25]

Chapter 3 focuses on King's spirituality as revealed in his sermonic prayers from 1954 to 1968. Here the discussion extends beyond King's private prayer life to his public prayer life, primarily in congregational settings. I examine in some measure his prayerful approach to reading Scripture and preaching. The chapter reveals that King never engaged in prayer-less preaching, or prayer-less sermonizing.[26] I highlight to some degree the space prayer occupied throughout his sermonic discourse as well as the dialogical character of his sermonic prayers. This approach has considerable merit, especially since King is known for his dynamic, effective, and gospel-centered preaching but not his poetic, picturesque, and moving sermonic prayers.[27] These prayers yield rich insights into King's public life and his sense of radical public piety. King's mode of pastoral prayer from 1954 to 1968 is the subject of chapter 4. The central argument I advance here is that King approached his role as pastor in a prayerful attitude and that he personified pastoral prayer in its purest form.[28] I explore in some depth King's view that pastoral conversation takes many forms, from proclamation to moral discourse to the act of praying itself. I also consider on some levels the ways King utilized prayer in his pastoral and priestly functions, another topic that awaits careful treatment by scholars.

Because King functioned in congregational contexts, his pastoral prayers, as chapter 4 shows, often assumed the form of communal or collective public prayer. Apparently, King understood that part of his responsibility as a pastor involved leading congregational prayers. I examine to some extent his stress on prayer as a resource in the collective experience of worship. It becomes clear that King always approached public prayer in a pastoral demeanor and spirit, regardless of the context.

King's practice of prayer during mass meetings, boycotts, street demonstrations, and other civil rights activities in the period from 1955 to 1968 is the topic of chapter 5.[29] This chapter explains how prayer became a wellspring of power and inspiration for King personally and for the movement he led. It tells us much about King's prayerful mood in the midst of struggle, about his reliance on prayer as a stabilizing and reenergizing force, and about the model of ministry that characterized his activities as a civil rights leader. The contention here is that King's movement prayers arose out of, and indeed modeled, a practical spirituality and that this practical posture in prayer made it impossible for him to divorce spirituality from ethical responsibility and social transformation.

The sixth and final chapter highlights the relevance of King's prayers and prayer life for people of faith today. It concludes that King's spiritual legacy is meaningful today, especially when considered from the standpoint of his attitude toward and experiences with prayer. In an age when the faithful are experimenting with prayer in different forms and arenas, King's prayer life remains a spiritual resource and a model for reflection. To be sure, King's prayer life actually affords lessons about how to become authentic and inspiring voices of faith and praise in a rapidly changing world.

The discussion that follows is based on a careful reading of King's private and public prayers, as he himself recorded them. I have filtered those sources in order to distill what they tell us about King's inward spiritual journey as a student, preacher, pastor, prophet, and civil rights activist.[30] King ultimately emerges not as some spiritually misguided and excessively pious figure but as a man with vibrant and unique spiritual gifts. *Never to Leave Us Alone* plumbs the depths of those gifts while opening a window into the soul of this phenomenal figure.

AN INWARD JOURNEY
IN THE WELLSPRINGS
OF THE BLACK PRAYER TRADITION

I prayed every day all day long, in a big, open field that was just being opened up as new ground, for three weeks.
—Ex-slave[1]

Each of us, in his own way, finds the stairs leading to the Holy Place.
—Howard Thurman[2]

Men always have prayed and men always will pray.
—Martin Luther King Jr.[3]

The prayer life of Martin Luther King Jr. was rooted in spiritual values and cultural traditions that extended back generations in America and many more in Africa. King's forebears brought the concept and habit of prayer to these shores as early as the 1600s. They prayed for deliverance in countless African languages, as they experienced a common horror in the bellies of slave ships; on the auction blocks; and in the cotton, rice, and tobacco fields in the New World.[4] The ancestral past was revered largely through prayer, and the art and discipline of prayer became one of the key markers of black faith. King drank from the wellsprings of this black prayer tradition while also enlarging it in the context of a movement for freedom, justice, and human community.[5]

The foundation for much of King's understanding of prayer was actually laid by slaves on the plantations of the American South. Imbued with a deep sense of the sacred, the slaves never thought of prayer as dogmatic prose or outdated ritual, and they refused to reduce the practice of praying to a mere exercise in exhibitionism or to some meandering attempt to appease God and impress believers. They variously referred to prayer as "talking with God," "ringing up heaven," "kneeling and bowing before the throne of grace," and "taking one's burdens before the Lord," and phrases like "praying in the spirit" and "laying the soul bare before the Lord" were commonly heard in the slave quarters.[6] This kind of language and thinking about prayer were passed down from generation to generation, thus becoming a critical component of what Lawrence W. Levine calls "the orally transmitted expressive culture" of African Americans.[7]

Undoubtedly, from the time of his birth in Atlanta, Georgia, in 1929, King was exposed to the most pervasive cultural images and conceptions of prayer as forged by slaves. This would not have been unusual in his case, especially in light of the presence of ex-slaves and their immediate descendants throughout the state of Georgia during his childhood. Through his devout parents, Martin Luther King Sr. and Alberta Williams King, and his saintly grandmothers, Delia Lindsay King and Jennie C. Parks Williams, King had his most direct exposure to that prayer tradition that first found expression in the wilderness of slavery.[8] Thus, it is not surprising that King himself would speak of prayer as conversing with God, crying out to God, taking problems to the Lord, or bowing before the God of the universe.[9] Clearly, there are echoes here of what the slaves and generations of their descendants had in mind when they sought to define and/or describe prayer and the experience of praying.

King's ancestors never doubted the necessity of prayer as a vital part of daily life. Prayer for them was much more than the heart and soul of religion, or an essential aspect of spirituality; it was a necessary ingredient in the total experience of living. In other words, the need for vigorous and earnest prayer—as adoration, confession, intercession, petition, and thanksgiving—never faded, because the slaves lived with a profound sense of their own finitude and inadequacy, of the unspeakable sorrow that clouded their daily existence, of their utter dependence on God, and of the need to thank God for the many blessings bestowed on them despite the pain of bondage. Significantly, they emphasized prayer in sermons and tales and often through the prism of song:

> Pray for me, pray for me,
> When you go to the altar,
> Please, please don't forget to pray for me.[10]

And

> Pray all de member, O Lord!
> Pray all de member,
> Yes my Lord!
> Pray a little longer, O Lord![11]

And there were these lines, marked by the pulsing rhythms of the heart and the most inspired voicing of faith:

> Pray on, pray on;
> Pray on dem light us over;
> Pray on, Pray on, de union break of day.[12]

Though King seldom specifically addressed prayer as an indispensable element in the lives of the slaves, his many reflections on slave religion in general are the best indication of his thoughts on the subject.[13] King knew that prayer was the channel through which so many of his forebears' wants and needs were met—that prayer, in the most striking ways, helped them to cope with what would have otherwise been unbearably painful episodes in their collective experiences as a people. King also saw prayer serving essentially the same purpose for blacks who, in his own time, still endured discriminatory policies and practices not far removed from slavery,[14] and his "fervent desire" was that they too would always "place prayer in a practical perspective."[15] Apparently, this larger black experience, as it unfolded across generations, was the basis for King's understanding of prayer as the lived theology of his people.[16]

The question of *what* slaves actually prayed *for* is equally significant for evaluating the black prayer tradition and King's place in it. The typical image of slaves praying for conversion, sanctification, and salvation in the afterlife[17] conveys only a part of the story. To be sure, the prayers of slaves focused on the ultimate concerns of life, but never to the neglect of their proximate needs and basic necessities. More specifically, they prayed for food, shelter, garments to cover their bodies, and the gift of life, always thanking and praising God that their beds were not their cooling boards, that their bed covers were not their winding sheets, and that the walls of their cabins were not the walls of their grave. They prayed as they "followed the drinking gourd 'on the Underground Railroad,' " when their families, friends, and loved ones were ripped apart by the slave trade, and whenever they felt the sting of the lash.[18] They thanked God for bringing them through "the seen and the unseen," and petitioned God for the strength to endure hardship, the will and the courage to struggle against injustice, and deliverance from captivity.[19] King would later mirror this kind of practical approach to praying as he thanked "God for sleep," for "waking me up this morning," and for the "miracle" of life.[20] Also in the tradition of his forebears, he prayed for family, friends, loved ones, and his people as a whole, for faith and fortitude in the midst of struggle, and for the dawning of freedom and justice.[21] Obviously, this manner of praying established a pattern that remained essentially unbroken in African American religious life, from the slaves and their immediate offspring down to and beyond King's generation.

But the forgers of this tradition never limited prayer to a mere expression of profound longings for the fulfillment of basic personal and communal needs. For people facing awful, traumatic experiences and unimaginable sorrow, prayer was a restless yearning for answers to the larger question of *meaning*, the *why* of the black experience. Simply put, prayer was a quest for meaning, as so often evidenced by the rich expressions in the voices and on the faces of those who prayed. Significantly, the slaves persevered in prayer even when answers from God seemed slow and far-fetched. Their prayer accounts bear eloquent and moving testimony to the resilience of the human spirit in the face of seemingly unending cycles of meaninglessness and tragedy. They also display a marvelous capacity on the part of slaves to heal themselves through the activity of praying, a capacity not particularly surprising in a culture in which prayer and healing rituals were coextensive. King's own quest for meaning and healing drew on the resources of this heritage, and it explains why he felt that slave religion had much to teach about how to deal with the tragic events of everyday life.[22]

The many contexts in which prayers were uttered, shared, and reshared reveal much about how this tradition developed over time. For enslaved Africans in the antebellum South, the "invisible institution"—clandestine meetings held in the fields, woods, thickets, ravines, and cabins—constituted the most prominent setting for both private and communal prayer.[23] In such settings, the slave preacher was often accorded an important role as prayer leader, and the potent character of prayer was never inconspicuous, as the cries of the heart burst forth in ardent flames of uninhibited expression. Some slaves preferred their own "regular praying place" or "praying ground," where they could, in the words of the spiritual, "steal away to Jesus."[24] As a means of keeping "the sound of their voices from penetrating the air," some prayed with their heads in pots, turned upside down, while others huddled behind thoroughly wetted quilts and rags.[25] King undoubtedly learned about such practices through his father and other elders, and they most certainly influenced his view of his own spiritual struggle and of his place in the larger sphere of African American religious culture.[26]

In the invisible institution, praying came together with preaching, testimony, shouting, and the singing of the spirituals, thus supporting King's view of the merging of the spiritual and artistic in traditional black life.[27] But prayer never followed a set of clearly defined liturgical forms or formal, written orders of worship. The informality of prayer became the standard as slaves communicated with God in verbal and nonverbal ways, and the prayers they recited orally were always spontaneous and extemporaneous. The invisible institution became the major wellspring of the black prayer tradition, prefiguring the visible, institutional black churches in that regard. The awesome silence that captured the mood as slaves prayed alone in secret places probably afforded much of the inspiration for spirituals, such as:

> Steal away, steal away to Jesus,
> Steal away, steal away home.
> I aint got long to stay here.[28]

And:

> An' I couldn't hear no body pray, O Lord,
> I couldn't hear no body pray, O Lord,
> O, 'way down yonder by myself,
> I couldn't hear no body pray.
> In de valley, I couldn't hear no body pray.
> On a my knees, I couldn't hear no body pray.[29]

King himself wrote about the "secret religious meetings" on the plantations, during which slaves "gained renewed faith" under the powerful and consolatory words of their preachers.[30] As one whose family history extended back to the slave era, King most certainly had some sense of how the experience of praying occurred in such meetings. Information concerning this aspect of the black religious past would have been accessible to him in the writings of scholars like W. E. B. Du Bois,[31] whom he read closely, and in the "interesting stories" he heard from his maternal grandmother, Jennie C. Parks Williams,[32] and other elders in Atlanta. Also, had King attended the average black Baptist church in Atlanta and especially in rural Georgia, which he most certainly did, he would have been exposed to the continuing impact of slave culture as it found expression in the prayer circle. His understanding of prayer as both personal and relational quite possibly benefited from what he learned about the values and traditions of the invisible institution.

Prayers offered in the context of family and community provided the foundation for King's spiritual and artistic bond with his predecessors. Communal prayer took place wherever and whenever slaves and their descendants gathered. Prayer meetings in the slave cabins and praise houses were a common practice.[33] Interestingly enough, public worship in churches, and especially white churches, afforded fewer opportunities for slaves to pray earnestly for the fulfillment of their personal and communal needs, especially since slave owners, overseers, constables, and other law officials were so often present. King knew and occasionally addressed the issue of the restraining effect that white presence had on black religious expression during slavery, but he also understood that the antebellum North, in which people of African descent had more freedom to develop and maintain separate and independent churches, presented a different situation.[34] It appears that the slave religious experience in the South and the phenomenon of the black church in the antebellum North came together in King's consciousness as he sought to grasp the spirit of unity and resistance that grew out of the prayerful struggle for survival and freedom.[35]

Had King studied slave culture in the upper South, and particularly in the border states of Delaware, Virginia, and Maryland, he would have discovered powerful examples of how the traditions associated with communal prayer carried over among the children, grandchildren, and great grandchildren of slaves. Slaves in these states actually came together annually with free Africans from the urban South and North for the Big August Quarterly, a religious festival that originated in Wilmington, Delaware, in 1813, and the prayer circle was always a central element in the festivities. Gatherings for the prayer circle in the African churches and on French Street in Wilmington were a common sight, as blacks prayed with all the strength of their voices, flinging their arms convulsively, nodding and bobbing their heads, and leaping to the point of exhaustion. The prayer leaders, forced to the center of the human ring, tended to be the most intense in their movements. Amazingly, the prayer circle frequently provided the impetus for slaves to escape to free territory, so it was never a practice linked only to the ritual life of people of African ancestry.[36]

In the decades after slavery, the prayer circle continued with all the power of its expression and appeal. At the 1882 gathering, "the most powerful singers and shouters took possession of the center of the floor" at the African Union Church, the focal point of the festival, and the singing gave "way to a short season of equally earnest prayer." Throughout the 1880s and 1890s, blacks gathered in "small circles," offering "stirring prayer in the sing-song manner peculiar to the race," as they also "frantically urged one another to more violent feats of gymnastic devotion, clapping their hands, jumping and shouting, and occasionally groaning."[37] Such practices survived through the first half of the twentieth century,[38] thus providing a model for the kind of prayer circle that would become characteristic of civil rights demonstrations in the 1960s. Although there is no evidence to suggest that King knew about the Big August Quarterly festivals, his own involvement in prayer circles would mirror much of the spirit of that tradition.[39] The relationship becomes all the more evident when one realizes that the prayer circle at Big August Quarterly celebrations, like that in King-led civil rights campaigns a century later, was usually linked to efforts to secure freedom for African Americans.[40]

The men and women who forged this tradition believed in the wonders of prayer, and they subscribed to a scriptural understanding that God heard and answered prayer. Describing prayer as "er sincere desire uv de heart," Henry Baker, born a slave in Alabama, declared that Jesus himself said "Ast whut yuh will en muh father will gib hit untuh yuh." He went on to assert that "prayah is sumpin dat unlocks de door."[41] The depth of this conviction was never undermined by the sense that God sometimes takes time in answering the pleas of the person who prays, for it was a common saying in the slave quarters that "He may not come when you want Him but He's always on time." The belief that God would answer prayer, fulfill the heart's desire, and supply needs was the inspiration for spirituals like:

> Oh, Jesus is on the main line;
> Tell Him what you want.
> Jesus is on the main line;
> Tell Him what you want.
> Jesus is on the main line;
> Tell Him what you want,
> Call Him up and tell Him what you want.
> If you want religion, tell Him what you want.
> If you want the Holy Ghost, tell Him
> what you want.
> If you're sick and you can't get well,
> Tell Him what you want.
> Call Him up and tell Him what you want.[42]

And there was the spiritual that follows, a statement pulsating with the determination to persevere in faith even when prayer offered few answers to the contradictions of life:

You can't make-a-me doubt Him,
You can't make-a-me doubt Him,
You can't make-a-me doubt Him,
in my heart.
I know too much about Him,
I know too much about Him,
I know too much about Him
in my heart.[43]

King would echo this concept of "the on-time God" who turns a listening ear to the cries of his children and "who makes a way out of no way."[44] Nurtured in a culture in which his people had long experienced the power of God unleashed in their lives through prayer, and in which the possibilities of prayer were essentially unquestioned, King would turn to prayer for answers that he knew he could not find elsewhere. When he declared the power of God to answer prayer, he was speaking out of a well-established and time-honored tradition.[45] As an heir of this tradition, he readily understood his elders' conviction that an indomitable faith constituted a part of that quality which gave efficacy to prayer and the experience of praying.[46]

This belief would become all the more evident after the Civil War and emancipation, even as changes of consciousness occurred in the prayers of ex-slaves and their descendants due to shifting social and political realities.[47] The Confederate defeat and emancipation fulfilled a prophecy the slaves had been praying for since the nation itself declared freedom from British colonial domination. "God planned dem slave prayers to free us like he did de Israelites, and dey did," declared former slave Alice Sewall.[48] The Alabama ex-slave Henry Baker vividly recalled those moments on his plantation when prayers broke out into praise and thanksgiving:

En Marse Harris say, "Yes, Jesse yuh is jes es free es I is en yuh kin go enywhere yuh wanna." En muh granddaddy come back en tole us en we all didn't hardly know what tuh do wid ourselves. Some left en some got togedder en had prayer meetin's in de house en prayed en thanked de Lawd fer d'liverance en ol' Ant Roney had a song. Aftuh we got free she sung it en we all he'ped her. We wuz all comin' fom prayer meetin' one night en she wuz shoutin' "Thank God we is all free."[49]

Similar images of newly freed slaves in prayerful celebration undoubtedly captured King's imagination in 1963, a hundred years later, as he, in his "I Have a Dream" speech in Washington, D.C., spoke of the Emancipation Proclamation as "a momentous decree" that became "a great beacon light of hope" and "a joyous daybreak" to "millions of Negro slaves," ending "the long night of their captivity."[50] Strangely enough, King's own prayerful spirit, as he celebrated civil rights victories and successful legislative initiatives in his own time, would recall, in some ways at least, the festive mood of his slave ancestors after emancipation.[51]

For the former slaves, the habit of praying for deliverance from captivity was largely replaced by prayer that sought God's guidance in the exercise of a new freedom. The ex-slave James L. Bradley of Arkansas reflected the sentiments of countless freed-persons when he prayed for the gift of learning, or that his "dark mind might see the light of knowledge."[52] The ex-slaves prayed for success in employment, for the security and stability of family life, for economic empowerment and self-sufficiency, for direction in building and maintaining their own churches and homes, and for wisdom in discharging the duties that came with their recently achieved civil and political rights. But the need to pray for freedom never really faded, as the Black Codes, Jim Crow laws, and mob violence against African Americans during the Reconstruction period signaled the establishment of yet another form of slavery. Consequently, the black prayer tradition was enlarged but not redefined or transformed, thus explaining why King was able to draw on it repeatedly and in profound ways.

Vital aspects of this tradition reached King through his family and home environment, the fellowship and artistic life of the black church, and the larger black community of Atlanta.[53] The seeds of King's emerging prayer life were actually planted from childhood in the King home and at Ebenezer Baptist Church, a congregation led by both his maternal grandfather and father, Adam D. Williams and Martin King Sr., both of whom were well-known Baptist preachers. As children, King Jr., his sister Christine, and his brother A. D. were required to pray at mealtime around the table, before departing for school, and at family prayer meetings on Sunday mornings. The youngsters were trained in the type of prayer life designed to instill and cultivate core Christian values. Here young King owed much to his parents, King Sr. and Alberta King, and to his maternal grandmother, Jennie C. Parks Williams, all of whom shared the King household on Auburn Avenue in Atlanta while he was growing up.[54]

Prayer meetings at Ebenezer Church, where the immediate offspring of ex-slaves could be found, were equally significant for King, affording a context in which he could learn the artistic side and intricacies of the prayer ritual. The dynamic, prayer-filled sermons of his father, affectionately called "Daddy King," were most certainly a source of both enlightenment and inspiration for King Jr.[55] It was in this setting that prayer intersected with preaching, singing, testimony, and shouting, thus recalling the religious culture of the slaves. The larger black community of Atlanta reinforced what King learned about prayer at home and at Ebenezer, for there were many in black congregations throughout Atlanta who modeled the kind of praying for which the slaves were known. It was in this larger black culture that King found precedent for his own prayer life. Steeped in the interrelated environs of home, church, and the larger black community, he was not likely to misuse prayer or to view it as simply some sacred indulgence or overly pious act inspired only by memory, habit, and tradition.[56]

King's own unique contributions to the black prayer tradition merit special attention if his rightful place in that tradition is to be fully understood. Significantly, King gave voice to vital aspects of the tradition as it unfolded among his slave ancestors while also remaining true to its genius and integrity. He reclaimed the language of freedom and deliverance in slave prayers as he prayed for the strength and wisdom needed for the continuing journey through the Egypt of slavery, the wilderness of segregation, toward the promised land of freedom, justice, and equality of opportunity.[57] King also honored that tradition by blending this-worldly and otherworldly concerns in his prayers, by stressing the idea of prayer as "talking with God," by highlighting the necessity of prayer, by extolling the wonders and possibilities of prayer, and by embracing a scriptural view that God answers prayer.[58] In short, folk praying and the black prayer tradition continued to live through King. In his prayers and prayer life, he echoed the heart desires, hopes, and dreams of his forebears.

King also expanded the black prayer tradition by making it useful in and relevant to a mass movement of nonviolent direct action.[59] Although prayer had always been a central ingredient for blacks involved in movements for social change, King and his followers were the first to make such a creative use of prayer in a church-centered, nonviolent crusade for freedom, justice, human dignity, and peace.[60] This was partly evident in the ways the prayer circle and the picket line were united in King-led civil rights campaigns. By infusing prayer into his nonviolent movement, King gave new meaning to prayer as creative energy and to the image of the black church as creative minority.[61]

King's contribution was equally evident in the diversity that characterized folk praying during civil rights crusades. In his "Message from Jail" (1962) in Albany, Georgia, which, unlike the Birmingham Jail letter, has been virtually ignored, King alludes to the importance of what he calls "prayer marches."[62] In other writings and speeches, he makes mention of "prayer vigils," "pilgrimages of prayer," "prayer campaigns," and "prayer rallies," all of which reflect his diversified and creative approach to praying and the prayer life.[63] This was clearly one of King's most innovative contributions to the spiritual side of the civil rights movement.

It should also be noted that many white people of different faith traditions had their first exposure to the traditions associated with folk praying through the movement King led.[64] The majority of whites who marched with King were unfamiliar with black church traditions as a whole, and white Protestants, Catholics, and Jews actually observed and participated with him in the prayer circle, prayer vigils, and prayer pilgrimages. This was especially the case with the so-called coalition of conscience in 1965 in Selma, Alabama, where some four hundred white religious leaders participated in the great march for voting rights. At the beginning of the march, the participants kneeled in a circle and Ralph D. Abernathy, King's assistant, offered a stirring prayer. In such settings, black prayer, for perhaps the only time in history, became a public and communal exercise involving blacks and whites of different faiths. By word and example, King actually pioneered in making prayer an engaging factor in advancing the spirit of interreligious dialogue and cooperation in the interest of justice, a contribution unprecedented for preachers and pastors in black church traditions.[65] King spoke to the historic significance of the occasion, calling it "the greatest and warmest expression of religious unity" in the "nation's history," and he delighted in the fact that this movement had occurred not in Rome but in the little town of Selma.[66]

The black prayer tradition explains why King approached life in a prayerful attitude. Although he was embarrassed as a boy by certain practices usually associated with praying in black churches, such as the shouting and stamping, he ultimately overcame this feeling and embraced the most vital aspects of that prayer tradition in its wholeness.[67] Undoubtedly, King's prayer life was intricately interwoven into the long history of people of African descent in the United States, and for him both the imperative to pray and the passion for praying emerged out of a deep consciousness of and identification with that history. The extent to which King embodied the genius of the black prayer tradition will become increasingly clear in the next chapter, which examines both his attitude toward prayer and his habit of praying while he was a student at Morehouse College, Crozer Theological Seminary, and Boston University.[68]

Martin Luther King engaged in a prayer circle with bystanders; Chicago,
1965. Credit: *John Tweedle from* A Lasting Impression, *University of South*
Carolina Press.

FROM SHADOWED PLACES

2

ECHOES OF PRAYER
FROM STUDENT DAYS, 1948–54

It would seem Satan had hidden the very object from my mind,
for which I had purposely kneeled to pray.
—Jarena Lee[1]

Not for myself I make this prayer, but for this race of mine, that stretches
forth from shadowed places, dark hands for bread and wine.
—Countee Cullen[2]

Prayer is indigenous to the human spirit.
—Martin Luther King Jr.[3]

Martin Luther King Jr.'s experiences as a student greatly influenced his approach to prayer in practical and intellectual terms. In the fall of 1944, at the tender age of fifteen, King enrolled at Morehouse College in Atlanta, Georgia, the institution at which both his father and maternal grandfather, Martin Luther King Sr. and Adam D. Williams, had matriculated. This predominantly black, all-male institution, which included a number of preacher-intellectuals on its faculty, appeared to be the ideal setting for a young man determined to grow spiritually and intellectually.[4] The Tuesday morning chapel services always began and ended with prayer, and students were encouraged to combine exceptional work in the classroom with a disciplined devotional life. At Morehouse, King had every opportunity to advance the prayer life he first embraced in the King home and at Ebenezer Baptist Church. But this would not occur without a spiritual and intellectual struggle. Having a questioning attitude toward religion from childhood,[5] King soon recognized an ineradicable disparity between the biblical fundamentalism he learned at Ebenezer and the theological liberalism to which he was exposed at Morehouse. When compelled to make a choice between the two, King turned naturally to liberalism, which would have lasting implications for his critique of the abuses and misuses of prayer.[6] Although he came to reject certain fundamentalist teachings, such as biblical inerrancy, the virgin birth, and the idea of a literal hell,[7] he never questioned the necessity and efficacy of prayer and praying. In fact, King's understanding of the power and possibilities of prayer remained essentially unchanged, and prayer continued to play a critical part in his daily spiritual journey. Largely due to the influence of Benjamin E. Mays, the Morehouse president, and George D. Kelsey, the professor of ethics, both of whom were "deeply religious" ministers familiar with "all the trends of modern thinking,"[8] King was able to keep his prayer life in proper perspective, even as he studied liberal theology, philosophy, and ethics.

King's continuing reliance on prayer for strength and guidance was virtually assured when he felt the call to ministry during his senior year at Morehouse.[9] From that point, prayer figured prominently in both his personal life and his preaching. King Sr., or "Daddy King," though concerned about King Jr.'s increasingly liberal stance on theological matters,[10] expected as much and more from his son, who occasionally prayed and preached at Ebenezer, and who often traveled with his father to country churches in rural Georgia where the spirit at prayer meetings swelled and overflowed into joyous shouts. At this point, the values and traditions of the King family, Ebenezer Church, and the larger black church culture of Georgia came together in King Jr.'s consciousness with the spiritual and intellectual influences at Morehouse College.[11] These sources together undoubtedly informed the content of King's prayers and shaped much of his approach to the art and activity of praying.

King Jr.'s work in the pulpit with his father at Ebenezer lasted until August, 1948, when he left for Crozer Theological Seminary in Chester, Pennsylvania. As assistant minister, the youngster most certainly would have given the invocation or offered other prayers that Daddy King deemed appropriate for a minister of his age and experience.[12] But unfortunately, none of King's public prayers from that Morehouse period have survived in written or recorded form, thus making it impossible to make precise claims about what he actually prayed *for* and *about*. The lack of such sources might be easily explained; King was not ordained in Christian ministry until February, 1948, some four months before he graduated from Morehouse. It is also doubtful that prayers from those last months at Morehouse ever even existed in any abundance. However, the fact that King was accepted as an assistant minister[13] is perhaps the best indication that the content of his prayers and his style of praying met with the approval of and was thus similar to King Sr. and other elders at Ebenezer, who were apt to prefer informal, extemporaneous prayers over formal, liturgical prayers, which would have been written out.

A prayer King offered during a wedding ceremony in August, 1948, some two months after graduating from Morehouse, has been discovered, and there is reason to believe that it provides clues to King's attitude toward prayer and manner of praying as a college student. King is believed to have given the prayer at the wedding of Samuel P. Long and Ruth Bussey at the Thankful Baptist Church in Decatur, Georgia, and it became his standard prayer when presiding at such ceremonies. The prayer combines a range of attitudes, especially adoration, intercession, and petition. King praised God as "the originator of all life" and the being whose "presence brings happiness to every condition"; he prayed for the couple's immersion in "the great harbor of peace, happiness and oneness"; and he asked for God's guidance in making their marriage "a creative activity" and an "exciting venture."[14] King's sense of prayer as communion with God and as an expression of creaturely dependence on God could not have been more evident at that particular point in his life. Clearly, he had come to understand prayer as something more than simply inspired speech or religiously informed rhetoric.[15]

Several of the prayers King recited in the period from 1949 to 1954, while he was in seminary and graduate school, exist in written form, and they reveal a prayer life gradually maturing over time.[16] Public worship was the setting for essentially all of these prayers, for King had by that time established a reputation as a bright young minister who spoke at churches and church-related functions in cities and towns throughout the country. Most of King's prayers were uttered in black churches, among people who were either uncomfortable with or unaccustomed to the use of prayer books. Some of the prayers are strikingly brief, consisting of only one or two sentences, but they are no less revealing of the thoughts and language of young King's head and heart. The prayers reveal a humble and contrite spirit, one who encountered the infinite holiness, majesty, and perfection of God; who confessed his own sinfulness and inadequacy; who prayed on behalf of individuals, groups, and the world; and who gave thanks for the basic necessities of life. Prayer became King's way of expressing himself to God, of experiencing God's presence and companionship, and of witnessing on behalf of others.[17]

Apparently, the habit of offering what might be called brief prayer lines in the course of sermons and speeches would remain typical of King throughout his student days at Crozer and Boston as well as during his public life and career as a minister and social activist. While there was always a prayer in his heart and on his lips, he rarely recited lengthy prayers in any context, including the church. In this regard, he was unlike many of the preachers and laypersons in his own church tradition, who, when "caught up in the spirit," would pray for long periods of time. For King, the content and sincerity of prayer could be conveyed in short as well as long prayers.[18]

After delivering a sermon titled "Mastering Ourselves" in June, 1949, at Ebenezer Baptist Church in Atlanta, King, then a student at Crozer, prayed for the ability always to choose the "good self" while mastering the "evil self."[19] At the close of another sermon titled "Civilization's Great Need," he prayed for a world without war, a more equitable "distribution of wealth," and "a brotherhood" not restricted by "race or color."[20] As was the case with his father and generations of other black preachers before him, King developed the habit of praying at the beginning and the end of his sermons, and his prayers, even in those early years, reflected not merely an intense desire for his own personal growth but also a deep yearning for a just, inclusive, and peaceful world.

Having been taught that prayer is both personal and relational, King never reduced it to a mere cry for the fulfillment of selfish needs and desires. Put another way, he took seriously the intercessory nature and social significance of prayer. His prayers show that he was socially conscious and had a sense of social responsibility even in his late teens and early twenties, long before he was catapulted to national and international fame in Montgomery. Furthermore, King's student prayers, considered in conjunction with those he uttered later, in the more active period of his life, prove that he always had a religious self-understanding and that he never separated personal piety from social transformation.[21]

While a graduate student at Boston University, pursuing a Ph.D. in philosophical theology, King gave a series of prayers prepared specifically for radio broadcasts in Atlanta. At that time, he was still spending summers at Ebenezer with his father, assisting as an associate minister. In one prayer, given in August, 1953, after a sermon called "First Things First," King urged the listening audience to "Seek ye first the Kingdom of God and His righteousness and all these other things shall be added unto you" (Luke 12:31). For King, seeking the kingdom of God meant "placing love, justice, and mercy first," as a way of realizing the fullness of an inner and outward peace.[22] During the summer and fall of 1953, King offered six prayers during a series of radio broadcasts from Atlanta's Ebenezer Baptist Church. In one prayer he acknowledged humanity's tragic tendency to revolt against God and asked for the will and the capacity to love both God and neighbor. Petitions for forgiveness course through these prayers, and one detects the cry for a pure heart and the spirit of perseverance in the search for truth and beauty in their most authentic expressions.[23]

King's prayers as a seminarian and graduate student reveal the continuing influence of a range of sources, aside from the Bible, on his spiritual life. Experiential and cultural influences, filtered largely through his extended family, Ebenezer Church, and other black congregations, took on added significance for him. King continued to offer prayers at Ebenezer,[24] and he occasionally prayed before African American congregations in the Northeast while fulfilling course requirements at Crozer and Boston. While at Crozer, King assisted J. Pius Barbour at Calvary Baptist Church in Chester, Pennsylvania, and in Boston he shared the pulpit with William H. Hester of Twelfth Baptist Church. Both congregations consisted of large numbers of black migrants from the South. These connections virtually assured King's continuing exposure to the most vital elements of the black prayer tradition. Much of his prayer life, and his clerical career as a whole, would follow the models that his father, Barbour, and Hester provided for him.[25]

But King's prayer life also owed much to his studies in liberal Christian theology and ethics. Of special significance in this regard was his exposure to the Social Gospel and Boston Personalism. The Social Gospel, to which King was exposed extensively at Crozer by Professor George W. Davis, reinforced his belief that prayer should deal with the both the celestial and earthly spheres. In other words, it should address not only humanity's ultimate concern but its preliminary concerns as well.[26] This is why King's student prayers speak so profoundly of the need to eliminate racism, poverty, violence, and other social conditions that damn the soul on earth while also highlighting the necessity for the transformation of the soul and uniting it with God in heaven. Moreover, the Social Gospel influence explains why King, in those early years, prayed earnestly for the desire and the strength "to unselfishly serve humanity."[27]

King's encounter with Boston Personalism grounded his conviction that the God to whom he prayed was neither abstract nor remote but personal, intimate, and immediate. His studies with personalists such as Edgar S. Brightman and L. Harold DeWolf[28] also strengthened his belief that God answered his prayers, that he had cosmic companionship, and that prayer has a role in the fulfillment of God's rational and loving purpose in the universe.[29] Furthermore, the content of King's prayers during and after his work at Boston reflect the influence of the personalist conception of the dignity and worth of all human personality and of the need for persons to live in community.[30] In fact, the influence of personalism and the Social Gospel was evident whenever King sought to explain prayer in spiritual and intellectual terms. The extent to which his spiritual life drew on these and other intellectual sources is all the more remarkable when one realizes that the culture in which he was nurtured too often viewed advanced education as an obstacle to genuine spirituality, a culture in which uneducated preachers boasted that their ministries had not been tainted by highfalutin, newfangled ideas. In his own prayer life, King was able to strike a proper balance between his experiential-cultural sources and his academic-intellectual influences. In this sense, he epitomized the genius of the black prayer tradition.

King wrote quite a bit about prayer during his years as a student, thus revealing the depth of his interest in the subject. In one of the few remaining academic papers from his Morehouse years, written on sacred and secular rituals, he identifies prayer as "a form of ritual." King, a college senior at the time, goes on to assert that "real religion" ends not with "a recitation of prayers," or "bowing before Him," but "by being pure and charitable" toward others.[31] Even at that point in his life, King was perceptive enough to keep prayer in proper perspective—viewing it as a means to an end and not an end in itself—while also exploring the larger question of what it really meant to be a person of faith in the world.

In a paper titled "The Significant Contributions of Jeremiah to Religious Thought," written in the fall of 1949 for Professor James B. Pritchard's Old Testament course at Crozer, King describes the prophet as "original in his exercise of prayer." He makes special references to Jeremiah's prayer for healing (Jer. 17:14) and his prayer for guidance against his enemies (17:18). Quoting from Jeremiah 12:1-3 and 17:14 and 18, and Robert F. Pfeiffer's *Introduction to the Old Testament* (1948), a recent publication, King calls Jeremiah "the father of true prayer, in which the wretched soul expresses both its subhuman misery and its superhuman confidence." Exploring Jeremiah's "inmost and intense communion with the Divine," King asserts that prayer for the prophet was not merely a "petition" or an "escape" from the harsh realities of daily existence. It was, rather, an "intimate" conversation with God, in which the prophet's "inner life" was exposed in all of its nakedness and with all of its perplexities, struggles, and temptations. King goes on to note that Jeremiah's prayers as revealed in 15:19 contain "the assurance" of answers from God. Although concerned with prayer as an aspect of Jeremiah's "mysticism" and "personal religion," King implies that prayer for the prophet also had some relevance in the sociopolitical arena, for it reflected a religion that did not "sanction the status quo."[32]

Although King would quote prayer lines from Isaiah, Habakkuk, and several other Hebrew prophets, in the paper on Jeremiah,

he expresses some uncertainty about how far these other prophets "went in the realm of prayer." He then notes how much of the
scholarship holds that "prophetic revelation" always came as an
answer to prayer. Clearly, King found in Jeremiah a "unique" and
"original" model for the healthy prayer life and also the prime
example for what prayer meant in the biblical-prophetic tradition.[33] Indeed, King's reflections on the mystical piety of Jeremiah
as exemplified in his prayer life is quite interesting, for they show
that the significance of the Hebrew prophets for King extended
beyond social and ethical considerations to embrace the personal
spiritual dimension as well.

In "How to Use the Bible in Modern Theological Construc-
tion," a paper he wrote for a course at Crozer called "Christian
Theology for Today," King makes an interesting comparison
between the Hebrew prophetic statement, "Let God speak with
us, lest we die," and Jesus' instructions concerning the Lord's
Prayer: "When ye pray, say, Our Father." In another paper for that
same course, written in February, 1950, King highlights Jesus'
"agonizing in prayer" under the shadow of "the Cross" as evidence of his humanity. King's essential point is that Jesus went
through the normal processes of human life and spiritual development, learning and expressing obedience and dependence on
God through the discipline of prayer.[34] Evidently, when King
wrote about prayer in the biblical tradition, he had both the Old
and New Testaments as a whole in view and not some particular
part of the Scriptures.

In a paper for Professor George W. Davis's philosophy of religion course, King, a senior at Crozer, writes about prayer as part
of the "religious phenomena" psychologists interpret. He stresses
psychologists' tendency to view prayer as the effort "to secure the
conservation of socially recognized values through 'an imagina-
tive social process,' " or "conservation between the ordinary ego of
the individual and the agency invoked."[35] Although it was rather
atypical of King to think and write about prayer in psychological
terms during those years, especially in view of his primary interest

in philosophy, ethics, and theology, this paper nonetheless reveal how far he was willing to go in order to understand prayer from an academic or intellectual standpoint.

In December, 1951, during his first year as a doctoral student at Boston University, King, in a philosophy of religion course with Edgar S. Brightman, explored the concept of prayer as "mystic insight," drawing on William E. Hocking's *The Meaning of God in Human Experience* (1912). Quoting Hocking, King declares that "the answer to prayer is whatever of simplicity, of naturalness, of original appreciation, is brought into our view of things by this act of obedience of the mind to its absolute object."[36] This paper was part of King's larger effort to examine Hocking's theistic absolutism in comparison to the finitistic theism of Brightman and J. M. E. McTaggart, the author of *Some Dogmas of Religion* (1906). Here King's brief comments on prayer are both philosophical and theological in nature, with some ethical implications.[37]

Some of King's writings at Crozer and Boston reflect his keen interest in the pragmatics of praying[38] and in the essentials of the disciplined prayer life. In one paper and outline, he probes deeply into the meaning of prayer, calling it "a throbbing desire of the human heart" and an "age-long and deep-rooted" yearning, maintaining that humans "always have prayed" and "always will pray." He flatly rejects conceptions of prayer as "irrational," "absurd," "presumptuous," and contrary to "natural law," and insists instead that prayer is a natural tendency, as native to "the human organism" as the rising sun is to "the cosmic order." King is convinced that "even the atheist" cries out at times "for the God" that his claims deny.[39] Clearly, the younger King approached questions regarding the meaning of prayer, prayer as "a native tendency," and the practicalities of praying with amazing instinct, depth of conviction, penetrating insight, and a high level of sophistication.

King's statement and outline, "The Misuse of Prayer," is perhaps his best treatment of the subject as a graduate student. Although prayer is "a natural outpouring" of the human spirit, he writes, "there is the danger" that human beings will use it "in an unnatural way." Here King cautions against making prayer "a substitute for work and intelligence,"[40] declaring that every human need, desire, and aspiration cannot be fulfilled through the habit of praying. He notes that knowledge of the great classics of culture, astronomy, and the creative discoveries in medical science came not directly through prayer but through the brilliance, hard work, and perseverance of great thinkers. King goes on to assert that those who "misuse," "abuse," or exploit prayer are apt to view God as some "cosmic bell hop" or "universal errand boy" who responds to every trivial human request and need. He further illustrates the point by referring to Exodus 14:10-15, where the Israelites, confronted with the Red Sea, are commanded by God to "Go forward,"[41] for God would not do for them what they were fully capable of doing for themselves. King would later explore the problem of "the misuse of prayer" at greater length, particularly as he sought to encourage human initiative and activism in the context of the civil rights movement.[42]

As evident in King's student papers, the question of what the believer should and should not pray for was central to his thoughts on the proper use of prayer. He praised the wisdom of praying for health, a charitable spirit, family, civil rights, and human welfare in general, but discouraged the idea of praying "for anything" that injures or destroys "somebody else." King insisted that one should never pray for God's help in exacting revenge against one's enemy, for one's own nation to win a war against another country, or for God to alter "the fixed laws" of nature and of "the universe." He highlighted the absurdity of white men praying for God's guidance and assistance in oppressing "the Negro,"[43] pointing once again to what for him was a callous abuse and exploitation of prayer for selfish gain. Praying as an act of selfishness was repulsive to King even in those early years, and he clearly suggested, especially in "The Misuse of Prayer," that prayer has a place in the struggle against hatred, intolerance, and war.[44] This is yet another indication that his concern for interracial community and world peace was first expressed not in Montgomery but in the classroom setting and in the papers he wrote during his years as a student.

King's paper, "The Misuse of Prayer," raises yet another concern with respect to the power, potential, and possibilities of prayer as a life-transforming force. He makes a fleeting reference to the need for believers always to be coworkers with God in ensuring answers to their prayers.[45] Remarkably, King, despite his youthfulness, had come to realize that persons who pray can truly expect answers only if they openly and actively prepare themselves for that for which they fervently pray. In other words, both divine grace and human initiative always come together in answers to prayers,[46] a position King would later emphasize repeatedly as he and his people struggled for much-needed social change.

Prayer was a sustaining force for young King in his studies, in his early spiritual formation, and in the embryonic stages of his ministry. He had a keen understanding of and deep commitment to the life of prayer, even as he immersed himself in the academy and in the marketplace of ideas. He never separated the yearnings of the heart from the life of the mind; both, in his estimation, contributed to the shaping of the human personality in its *wholeness*.[47]

The actual prayers King uttered as a student reveal much more than a young, precocious mind in search of the deeper meanings of prayer and the disciplined spiritual life. They also reflect a vibrant spirit and a perceptive personality fully embracing the sacred duty of prayer and grasping the richest results of praying. Moreover, these prayers provide a window into the soul of a young man who felt ordained by God to serve and who had come to believe he was an instrument of a special destiny, as it related to the freedom of his people.[48] Thus, one must begin with King's student prayers in order to comprehend the role of prayer as the power and mainspring of his life.

But the element that made King's approach to prayer and praying distinctively his own had to do with much more than just the formal training he received at Morehouse, Crozer, and Boston. His insights on prayer were shaped and nurtured by the experiences of standing and praying in the pulpits of churches throughout the country. This will become more evident in the following chapter, which explores the content, meaning, and impact of prayers King recited in the process of preaching and/or sermonizing.[49]

King in a prayerful mode during his final hours in Memphis, 1968.
Source: UPI/Corbis.

TREMBLES IN THE BREAST |3
PRAYER AND THE ART
OF PREACHING, 1954–68

> *Prayer is the soul's sincere desire, uttered or unexpressed;*
> *The motion of a hidden fire, that trembles in the breast.*
> —James Montgomery[1]

> *Never rest easy till you feel in you a change*
> *wrought by the Holy Spirit.*
> —Lemuel Haynes[2]

> *In Him there is feeling and will, responsive*
> *to the deepest yearnings of the human heart.*
> —Martin Luther King Jr.[3]

Prayer was a central element in the proclamations and Christian witness of Martin Luther King Jr. Simply put, he was a praying preacher who approached the art of preaching and/or sermonizing in a prayerful spirit. Indeed, prayerful preaching is the key to understanding King as a master pulpiteer, and it explains much of the power and creativity he brought to his sermonic discourse and to his art as one who proclaimed the Word as revealed in Scripture. Moreover, King's passion for praying and devotion to the gospel message accounted in great measure for his worldwide appeal and effectiveness as a preacher.[4]

Convinced that the ability and energy to preach came from God, King made prayer an all-commanding factor in his sermon preparation.[5] His sermons always began and took shape in his head and heart as he prayerfully surrendered to God, and he routinely prayed before committing his sermons to paper and delivering them in the pulpit. This habit of prayer became more structured when King became the pastor of the Dexter Avenue Baptist Church in Montgomery, Alabama, in April, 1954. The young pastor usually spent at least fifteen hours a week preparing his Sunday sermon, and it was through the discipline and activity of prayer that he actually learned how to preach.[6]

The claim that prayer made King a preacher is easy to sustain on the basis of King's own account of an experience he had at the very beginning of the Montgomery bus boycott in 1955–56. Unanimously chosen in a hastily called meeting to head the Montgomery Improvement Association, the organization brought into being to lead the boycott, King had only twenty minutes to prepare for "the most decisive speech" in his life. Overcome by feelings of anxiety and inadequacy, and needing God's "guidance more than ever," King turned to prayer, asking God to restore his balance and to be with him in that trying hour. The young preacher went on to speak "without manuscript or notes," and the presentation "evoked more response than any speech or sermon" he had "ever delivered," thus reinforcing his conviction that God answers prayer and that God's responses are always on time.[7] King also came to better understand what "the older preachers" in the black church meant when they declared, "'Open your mouth and God will speak for you.'"[8]

King's experience of God's power in that critical moment also yielded other insights about his prayer and preaching and the relationship between the two. The power of his message on that particular occasion reflected the intensity of his private prayer life. From that point, King was more intentional about praying in the privacy of his home, church office, hotel room, and other relatively isolated places in which he found a greater measure of peace, silence, and solace.[9] King also came to a better understanding of the relationship between private, spontaneous prayer and impromptu, extemporaneous preaching. This could not have been more important for one who did as much and perhaps more preaching than any other clergyman in his time. Although King, due to his habit of careful study and prayerful preparation, was not one to accept a preaching engagement on the spur of the moment,[10] there were indeed times when he was called on to fill in for his father, King Sr., on short notice, and at such times he benefited greatly from what he learned about private prayer and extemporaneous sermonizing.

Mervyn A. Warren has noted King's "dependence on preparatory prayer" in thinking through and writing his sermons. According to Warren, "faith in God expressed through prayer consistently preceded and accompanied King's gathering and assessment of sermon materials." King's appointment book "shows that two to three days each week were set aside for special 'Prayer and Meditation,'" as part of a routine in sermon preparation. Also, King remained in a prayerful mood from the point of sermon preparation to the time he ascended the pulpit. Warren, who sat in the pastor's study with King as King prepared to deliver a sermon at the Central United Methodist Church in Detroit in 1966, recalls the spirit of prayer that pervaded the scene: "Before leaving the pastoral study for the pulpit, King and fellow clergymen bowed in prayer. For what, precisely, did they pray? Their petitions were for God to bestow upon King, the preacher of the hour, power and physical strength and effective oral persuasion to meet the hearers' needs."[11]

King's sermons always began and ended with either a verbal or silent prayer, in part because this was expected in black churches, the contexts in which he most often preached. Before preaching, he sometimes sat silently in a chair in the pulpit with his eyes closed and hands folded underneath his chin; on other occasions he either knelt in secret prayer in the pulpit, bowed his head while seated, stood in a prayerful attitude and posture, or

uttered a prayer publicly before the congregation before reading
a passage from Scripture and announcing the subject of the sermon he planned to preach. For King, prayer before the sermon
was significant for a number of reasons. In one sense, prayer was
his way of displaying his openness and vulnerabilities before God,
of allowing his soul to ascend to self-forgetting adoration, and of
preparing himself for a task for which he felt essentially unwor-
thy, despite his call by God to preach.[12] Put another way, prayer
became a matter of invoking the supernatural and an expression
of his humble submission before the omnipotent, omniscient,
omnipresent, and omni-benevolent God, without whom preaching becomes a meaningless play of words.

Prayer at the beginning of the sermon was equally significant
for King in that it evoked a sense of divine presence and the anointing and empowering that come with the Holy Spirit. This involved
creating a favorable atmosphere for the preaching of the gospel,
so that the word of God could be both proclaimed and received
in the right attitude and spirit. Steeped in the traditions of the
black church, King instinctively knew that this required fervent
and soul-searching prayer, the kind of praying that allowed space
for the working of the wonders of God's power in the midst of the
proclaimed Word.[13] It was here that the prayer of faith figured so
prominently in King's preaching.

King also began his sermons with prayer as a way of establishing his authority to do what God had called and equipped him to
do; namely, to preach the Word of God. Although he took seriously the universal priesthood of believers, which speaks to the
need for every person of faith to minister in some fashion, he was
convinced that the preacher had a divine gift that came directly
from God in a personal religious experience.[14] Therefore, the
person who "stands in the shoes of John"[15] must establish himself
through prayer before actually preaching. King had learned from
his father, King Sr., and other older ministers, that praying preachers are God's agents for "declaring the truth between the living and
the dead."[16]

On yet another level, prayer before the sermon helped King to proclaim the good news in a spirit of consecrated fearlessness and freedom. He insisted on a kind of holy boldness in the pulpit, and he refused to be inhibited with respect to what he uttered, especially when he was speaking truth to power. Here prayer and the prophetic role for King were interconnected. He lamented the fact that white preachers, especially in the South, talked so much about the power and necessity of prayer in their pulpits but were not free and courageous enough to preach in those same pulpits about the evils of racism and segregation. King felt similarly about black preachers who, though "freer" and "more independent than any other person in the community,"[17] retreated into a posture of silence, complacency, and indifference when confronted with the need to stand up and preach an uncompromising gospel or one that challenged principalities and powers and evil in high places. In short, King saw that the praying, fearless preacher was expected, appreciated, and applauded in his own church tradition, and he consciously set out to reflect this to the fullest in his own prayer life and preaching art.[18]

King found his model for the relationship between prayer and prophetic preaching in the ancient Hebrew prophets and Jesus of Nazareth. Here he discovered powerful prophetic voices who were less concerned about the ritualistic and ceremonial aspects of the prayer life and related it more to the ethical and social concerns of life. King's prayers and prophetic warnings for a nation obsessed with racism, militarism, the victimization of the poor, and idolatry recalled the prophets' prayers and prophecy in a Hebrew society haunted by problems of social dislocation, the mistreatment of the poor and humble by the privileged, and the worship of false gods. King detected in Jesus' prayer life and parables concerning prayer a commitment to the type of altruistic love, undeserved suffering, and sacrificial servanthood that could redeem the soul of a nation and indeed all humanity.[19] In King's thinking, the vital dimensions of prophetic prayer and prophetic preaching were richly blended in the lives and ministries of the Hebrew prophets and of Jesus.

In King's case, prayer before preaching also ensured that what he proclaimed would first and foremost be pleasing and acceptable in the sight of God and, consequently, also meaningful and transforming for his hearers. King knew that sermons contradicting the will and purpose of God for humanity betrayed the call to preach, and this is why he shuddered at the very thought of pulpits being used to preach a gospel of bigotry and intolerance or to speak only to the inner spiritual needs of believers.[20] For him, the preacher had to pray for guidance to say what needed to be said and to proclaim what needed to be proclaimed. Moreover, prayer expressed the hope that what the preacher said would have a lasting, positive effect on the lives of listeners. The thought of sermons having the same effect as water on a duck's back, which is easily shaken off, bothered King immensely.[21]

King's habit of praying at the close of his sermons deserves special consideration as well. For him, prayer became a necessary footnote to the message of the sermon. It was also about asking God for direction in living out daily the truths he proclaimed, for he understood that the sermon was an exercise in futility if its impact remained confined within the consecrated walls of the church or if it failed to move both himself and his hearers to positive self- and societal transformation. In other words, prayerful preaching was for King a call to go out and change oneself and the world for the better and in the interest of the common good.[22]

It is clear from the foregoing discussion that King never engaged in prayerless sermonizing and/or preaching, and that prayer and preaching were inseparable in his mind. There is no other way to explain the space prayer occupied throughout his sermonic discourse. In a general sense, prayer for King was more than simply an indispensable part of preaching; his prayers became sermons and his sermons, to some extent, prayers, especially since his sermons were always peppered with short prayer lines.[23] Furthermore, King memorized some of his prayers, like his sermons, and repeatedly used them in one version or another in various contexts.

King was not known to recite formal prayers in the pulpit. In this sacred arena, rather, he usually prayed spontaneously and extemporaneously, and he offered his prayers in the presence of ordinary, praying church folk and in the context of a genuine spirituality and humility. King believed that in order to be effective, a praying preacher needed a praying congregation. He fully understood the difficulties of preaching to a prayerless congregation. For him, the sermon was the point at which a praying preacher communicated truth to a praying church. In fact, the Word of God could only be preached with the help of a praying church, for sermons in the black Christian tradition are actually preached with the participation of both the pulpit and pew.[24] This is how King made the prayer experience and the preached word such a vital and enriching element in the worship experience.

The dialogical character of the prayer and preaching moments was most evident in this cooperative exercise between the praying preacher and the praying congregation, and King knew and experienced this firsthand from the time he was in seminary and graduate school. In other words, King functioned in ecclesial circles where church folk prayed and preached along with him, punctuating his sermons with cries of "Lord have mercy," "Lord help him," "Have mercy, my God," and "Tell the story."[25] The activity of prayer, like the sermon itself, was always a dialogue and never a monologue. The black church was central to King's capacity to master both prayer and preaching as dialogue.[26]

But prayer was only one of the many approaches King used to encourage lively and dramatic responses from church people. On some occasions, he began his sermons with what in the black preaching tradition is called "an apology," during which he apologized for not feeling well, hoarseness, or some other disability. His purpose was to drive home the point, rather indirectly, that he was

compelled by his call to preach at any cost and that the congregation should pray with him a little while.[27] At such times, King was
known to preach some of his very best sermons, as his listeners
urged him on with cries of "preach anyhow," "Be with him, Jesus,"
"Lord help him," and other expressions of ecstasy.

At other times, King began his sermons by reflecting on
some transforming encounter he had had with God in the
midst of a crisis situation, a situation with which his black listeners could easily identify.[28] In language and tone familiar to
the folk, King might begin: "One day after finishing school I
was called to a little church in Montgomery, Alabama. Things
went well for a while, but one day, I had an experience at midnight, and you can have some strange experiences at midnight,"
and so on. The audience instinctively sensed what would follow
and responded freely and enthusiastically.[29] In such situations,
testimony helped create the climate for participative prayer and
preaching.

On other occasions, King turned to humor, joked with the
congregation, and made them laugh, thus relaxing them and preparing them for active involvement in both the prayer and the sermon. For example, he might announce his intention to be brief,
reminding the congregation that "brevity for a Baptist preacher is
a magnificent achievement."[30] After being introduced in glowing
terms at certain times before speaking, he sometimes told the story
of the old maid who was surprised to hear she was getting married
and responded by thanking God for the rumor. "I know all of these
marvelous things you heard about me are not true," he would say,
"but thank God for the rumor."[31] On still other occasions, King
amused his audience by referring to the problems and uneasiness
he and his aides experienced while flying to their different destina-
tions, noting that he had "faith in God in the air," but "had more
experience with him on the ground." "I would rather be Martin
Luther King late," he added, "than the late Martin Luther King."[32]

Such humorous anecdotes were also designed to assist in
establishing the mood for dialogical prayer and preaching. It never

diverted the folk from the rich, profound, and serious nature of King's prayer, and sometimes it was connected to the theme and general thrust of his sermon. The point is that humor created among King's listeners a responsive mood, thus making it possible for his prayers and sermons to become theirs as well. King's skillful use of humor and other devices as a means of connecting with his church audiences was most certainly one indication of the high levels of ingenuity and creativity he brought to his preaching art—ingenuity and creativity that established him, along with his father and generations of preachers before him, "as a fashioner and exemplar of culture."[33]

The content of King's sermonic prayers should be examined more closely for what they share concerning not only his prayer life but also the larger core of his convictions, vision, value system, and ethics. Strangely, scholars have not taken these sources seriously, even those who explore the rhetorical significance of King's sermonic language,[34] his preaching to black congregations,[35] the cultural and spiritual resonances of his sermons,[36] and his African American preaching voice and pulpit presence.[37] This inattention to King's sermonic prayers is indefensible in view of his own claim that he was "fundamentally a clergyman, a Baptist preacher."[38]

King's sermonic prayers disclose much about his religious self-understanding. Apparently, he felt obligated to, among other things, use the pulpit and the sermon in corporate worship to promote a ministry of prayer. This prayer ministry, as King saw it, was designed to invite reflection, to encourage meditation, and to challenge church folk to come to terms with their own calling as persons of faith and as ambassadors of God's word as recorded in the Bible.[39] He knew that spreading the good news of the gospel should involve the whole people of God, and he prayed with hope that those who listened to him would also become, in their own unique ways, bearers and proclaimers of the profound truths of Scripture.[40]

At the same time, King's sermonic prayers reflect a vivid awareness of the essential sinfulness of humanity and of the essentiality and priority of divine grace. While affirming the importance of self-acceptance, self-esteem, and the dignity and worth of all human personality, King, in his prayers and sermons, insisted nonetheless that pride and self-centeredness are never paths to God. In his thinking, prayerful preaching made possible the atmosphere in which human frailties and the imperfections of human nature could be exposed and earnestly expressed, and in which the forgiving, healing, and transforming power of God's grace could be realized and experienced.[41]

But one also detects in King's sermonic prayers the heart and soul of a committed churchman who felt compelled to point the faithful toward a higher spirituality and morality. In the middle of a sermon titled "Living Under the Tensions of Modern Life," King declared that "the great prayer of life" should always speak to the need to make life creative and productive, the very best that it could possibly be. For King, reshaping life through the art and exercise of both prayer and preaching remained a most cherished value, as a careful study of his sermonic prayers shows.[42]

From another standpoint, sermonic prayers added a dimension to King's ministry that made him all the more effective in motivating and mobilizing people for social change. He always shared his prayers with the hope that every rational and moral person who listened to him preach would also be empowered to become not only agents of truth but sacrificial servants in pursuit of social justice and peace. In other words, prayerful preaching resonated best with the human situation when it inspired believers to translate the gospel they heard and received in the pew into practical action and reality in the larger society. In one of his sermonic prayers, King called this "life's central test" or "the ultimate test of one's loyalty," and in another he suggested that this is always part of a "journey" on "the road of life."[43]

King was undoubtedly referring here to the cross every true believer must bear for the redemption and transformation of the human situation. Pointing to the preaching, prayers, and actions of Jesus Christ as the standard for all times, King maintained that every sacrificial life has its Gethsemane and Calvary but also its resurrection and redemption. Furthermore, he insisted on a culture of prayer and of preaching in which this dynamic was continuously conveyed in the most emphatic and unmistakable terms. The cross is a pervasive symbol in King's sermonic prayers, but it calls believers to a strikingly real and quite demanding mission.[44] In short, the Christian life for him amounted to an inescapable pilgrimage in cross-bearing and redemptive suffering for the common good. This is also how King understood "love in action."[45]

Equally significant are the ways in which King employed prayerful preaching to challenge church folk regarding the need for brotherhood and community. The concern for "other selves," "the neighbor," and even "our enemy neighbors" is a prominent theme in his sermonic prayers. At the end of his sermon, "Paul's Letter to American Christians," King prayed for humans to see the need to cooperate with God in overcoming racial barriers.[46] Convinced that the power of prayer, much like that of preaching, is largely affected by the character and conduct of the person who prays, King suggested that the racist mind-set was as foreign to genuine prayer as it was to the to the larger demands of the Christian ethic.[47] Thus, he called for a new spirit of prayer and preaching invigorated by an unshakable determination to reconcile humans with each other and with the God who is the parent of all humankind.

In a more general sense, prayerful preaching in the Kingian mode reflected a broader quest for "a new humanity" and "a new world." In pulpits across the globe, he prayed for the coming of a new world order. Put another way, prayer and preaching for him had to be solidifying and transforming forces in the largest sphere of human existence, especially if the disjointed structures of an interrelated reality are to be forged into a harmonious whole.[48] King's sermonic prayers were always directed outward and were never merely confined to his own needs or those of his race and religion. In his mind, prayerful preaching had to be universal in its application and appeal in order to meet the test of relevance and time.[49]

King demonstrated by the power of his art that prayer gives character to preaching and to the Christian life as a whole. It was his conviction that stubbornly unrighteous and unjust persons could never make pure and meaningful supplication because ideas, feelings, and behavior always inform the practice of praying as much as preaching. Therefore, prayer and a clean spirit are the preacher's best and most durable weapons when faced with the perilous and capricious nature of life and human existence. This aspect of prayer could not have been more important for King, who constantly faced the threat of death.

Prayer and preaching for King were not mere shibboleths or meaningless expressions of the verbal art. In his estimation, both constituted the heart and soul of any authentic religious experience. Real praying for him translated into real preaching, and real praying and preaching translated into the ideal spiritual, moral, and social life. Moreover, whenever King ascended the pulpit to proclaim the Word, he spoke as one fully acquainted with the renewing and staying power of prayer.[50]

King's leadership was effective because his praying and preaching were effective. True leadership in his case made prayer and preaching indispensable, and he left a powerful legacy of both. In fact, prayer and preaching were the great factors in the sharing and spreading of King's gospel and vision of human freedom. He went from one setting to another to pray, but the prayers he recited in the context of his sermons carried a special meaning for those who saw God at work through his activities in history.

As a preacher, King's life was largely defined by his prayerful attitude and spirit. But his prayer life was never limited to his sermonic prayers, or to pulpit praying, for he literally lived by prayer. Prayer pervaded every corner of his life, and it also became a vital part of that controlling force that linked him to people of faith from virtually every station in life. This was most apparent in his prayer life as a pastor,[51] which is covered in some detail in the next chapter.

King takes time to pray during the planning for the March on Washington, 1963. Source: Jay Leviton, Atlanta.

BEFORE WHOM ANGELS BOW | 4
THE POTENCIES
OF PASTORAL PRAYERS, 1954–68

> *O thou King eternal, immortal, invisible, and only wise God,*
> *before whom angels bow and seraphs veil their faces, crying*
> *holy, holy, holy, is the Lord God Almighty.*
> —Maria W. Stewart[1]

> *Prayer has therefore seemed a spasm of words*
> *lost in a cosmic indifference.*
> —George A. Buttrick[2]

> *It is faith in Him that we must rediscover.*
> —Martin Luther King Jr.[3]

Martin Luther King Jr.'s prayer life as a pastor was shaped by the time he lived in, by the circumstances of his leadership in the church and in the civil rights movement, and by the range of spiritual and intellectual sources to which he continuously turned. These three factors—time, context, and sources—were especially relevant for King, who, perhaps more than any clergyperson before him, extended pastoral prayer beyond the narrow confines of traditional parish life to the broader public sphere, thus making pastoral prayer the inseparable accompaniment to his effort to redeem the soul of a nation. Patrick G. Coy is thus correct in noting that King was not simply a church pastor but "an American pastor" as well.[4]

King was thoroughly convinced that it took fervent and persistent prayer to pastor a church, and his own life bore the stamp
of that conviction. While serving as senior pastor of the Dexter
Avenue Baptist Church in Montgomery, Alabama, from 1954
to 1960, he not only preached at Sunday services, baptized new
members, served communion, led Bible study, met with church
organizations and auxiliaries, coordinated the congregation's pro-
gramming, visited the sick and shut-in, and officiated at funerals
and weddings, but he also sought to deepen his own conversation
and walk with God through prayerful reflections on life.[5] Faced
with enormous administrative and religious responsibilities and
challenges, and with agonizing moments of loneliness and uncertainty, King understood that his seminary training and intellectual gifts,[6] though necessary and significant, could not guarantee
what was called in black church circles "power from on high." This
view helps explain why King, in both his private and public lives,
mastered prayer as the art of pastoral conversation with God.[7]

King's roles as *religious leader* and *ritual leader* are perenni-
ally relevant to any serious discussion of how he utilized prayer as
a pastor. He understood that much of his pastoral responsibility
involved praying publicly and leading the congregation in prayer,
and this responsibility necessitated a strong private prayer life
as well. In other words, private prayer prepared King to become
the prayer leader in the context of corporate worship and in the
larger arena of congregational life. The pastor as prayer leader
in a congregation of pray-ers is what he envisioned for himself
and his people at Dexter. Though he never wrote a practical and
experience-based book about prayer for his congregation, he consistently reminded his parishioners that prayer is an essential and
vital part of the religious life.[8]

However, in stressing the importance of sustaining a life of
prayer, King had in mind prayer as a profound surrender of the self
to God, not prayer rooted in self-pride, self-righteousness, and self-
centeredness. He also taught his congregants that prayer is the cardinal principle of spirituality, an all-engaging force in the spiritual

life, and he proclaimed the legitimate and illimitable possibilities of prayer as adoration, supplication, thanksgiving, and intercession. King always reflected the need to be intentional in prayer, to communicate with the spiritual realm with an earnestness of heart, and to pray in practical ways about practical matters—in his own prayers before the congregation, and he often expressed the same in his preaching, moral discourse, counseling, and pastoral recommendations.[9]

In his capacity as religious leader, King prayed in various contexts at Dexter. The invocation, the pastoral prayer, and the benediction were part of his routine during worship services on Sunday mornings, and he recited prayers over tithes and offerings, at Wednesday night prayer meetings, at business meetings, during the administration of the sacraments, at Bible study, before church dinners, for the sick and shut-in, and at weddings, funerals, and other church events. King also prayed for Dexter and her membership, for the effectiveness of her programmatic initiatives, and for the success of her ministries and mission goals and priorities. In short, prayer became a vital part of King's caring function as a pastor.[10] Having observed his father, J. Pius Barbour, William H. Hester, and numerous other black pastors fulfill their responsibilities as prayer leaders, King was well situated to perform in this capacity, without any on-the-job training. Moreover, he had no barriers of style and feeling to overcome when relating his role as prayer leader to the larger sphere of his activities as a pastor.

King's role as *ritual leader* manifested itself specifically and most prominently in the ways in which he exercised not only the ministry of the Word and of the sacraments but also the art and discipline of prayer. Here the characteristic of "priesthood" in King's pastoral experience became quite evident.[11] In his priestly function, King related this world to the other world, mediating between the living and the dead in order to lessen the hardships for his congregants in this life, and prayer was central to this effort. Also, he constantly reestablished his parishioners' relationship with one another and with God through prayer; in this way, they could perceive themselves more clearly as the people of God. As a mediator between God and the church members at Dexter, King constantly pointed out where, when, and how the divine was present for them—in worship, Scripture, the black experience, society, and the world—and he demonstrated the divine presence and will not only in his attitude, actions, sacrifices, and preaching, but in his prayer ministry as well. In these respects, King's function as ritual leader or priest was identical to that of the slave priest, as described by W. E. B. Du Bois, James Weldon Johnson, and others.[12]

Called to serve a congregation that knew and experienced crucifixion daily, King refused to ritualize the act of prayer. His praying was designed to comfort and reaffirm his congregants at Dexter in the midst of their predicament and struggles. Through the spirit and discipline of prayer, King brought together his people's joy and sorrow, their thankfulness and longings, their concerns and pathos, and presented them before the altar of God's grace.[13] Furthermore, King's praying in this instance, much like his administration of the Lord's Supper, supported the ultimate calling of his parishioners to share fully in the sacrificial life of Jesus Christ himself.

As is the case with any ritual leader, King had a deep appreciation for contemplative prayer and of the potential of the Christian inner life, and he displayed this appreciation in his personal life, preaching, counseling, and pastoral demeanor and style while at Dexter. He taught and demonstrated that prayer for each congregant, including himself, should involve not only a search for the deepest ground of his or her identity in God, but also an intense longing for the simple presence of God, a deeper understanding of God's Word and commandments, and the will and capacity to listen to and obey God.[14] In this regard, solitary prayer was as important to King as communal or group prayer.

By urging his parishioners to steep themselves in the quiet character of prayer,[15] King in his capacity as pastor was not functioning outside of the religious and cultural sources that produced him, for there is a contemplative trajectory in the black prayer tradition that is not ecstatic and theatric. Echoes of this course through slave spirituals such as "Steal Away to Jesus," "Hush, Hush, Somebody's Calling My Name," "Hunting for the Lord," and "I Couldn't Hear Nobody Pray." King knew this well, and his idea of the heart's humble intercourse with God through silent prayer mirrored this heritage.[16] Furthermore, King consistently reminded the membership at Dexter that not merely prayer but the worship experience as a whole involves, at least on some levels, "silent communication with God."[17] In King's thinking, this acknowledgment did not amount to a categorical rejection of the more demonstrative elements of African American liturgical life.[18]

For King, the lives of the ancient Hebrew prophets and of Jesus highlighted the essentiality of contemplative prayer. He saw that the prophets and Jesus withdrew at times to quiet places to commune with God, thus becoming a model for every sincere believer.[19] King also understood that periods of quiet prayer and meditation were necessary for him and his church folk because of the pressures of black life in the South and the hectic pace and rapid change of modern life in a noisy world. Furthermore, contemplative prayer figured prominently in King's distinction between worship as "a public affair" and worship as "a private affair,"[20] and part of his role as priest or ritual leader was to teach the folk at Dexter that both were essential to the well-rounded spiritual life.

In order to better understand how King related the theoretical and the practical in the context of congregational life, we must consider on several levels the question of how he perceived and utilized prayer as a pastor.[21] In theoretical and practical terms, he saw prayer as a devotional act essential to the worship experience and liturgical life of the church, to be accompanied by preaching, music, scripture readings, and testimony.[22] Prayer for King was also a resource in worship for believers who wished to deepen both their own personal prayer lives and their experience of praying corporately with other believers. As one accorded an important role in worship as a prayer leader, he once again preferred extemporaneous prayers[23] and was not an advocate of praying in conformity with standardized ritual and liturgy. King relished the life of prayer and spent much time praying with his parishioners in worship.[24] His pastoral prayers at the Dexter Avenue Baptist Church moved people and were effective because he spent quality time with his parishioners in what he called "the valley" of life.[25]

In a real sense, King's pastoral prayers, much like his preaching, were designed to establish his own authority as a mouthpiece for God in the life of his congregation. This too is important when considering his understanding and practice of prayer as a pastor. King held that as pastor, he was the "central figure" around whom the ministry of Dexter revolved and that respect for his office and full cooperation with him were indispensable to the progress of the congregation, spiritually and otherwise.[26] In other words, King approached prayer and the prayer ministry at Dexter with the uncompromising conviction that his authority as pastor came directly from God,[27] and this alone elevated him to the unrivaled position of prayer leader. That authority was reinforced by the sincerity, power, eloquence, and grammatical profundity that he brought to the congregation's prayer ministry.

On another level, prayer served a didactic purpose for King as he sought to enlighten his congregation to the meaning, purpose, and possibilities of prayer. King gave practical lessons on the prayer life, and the subject most certainly came up in lectures at Dexter.[28] He felt that prayer should engage the heart and spirit as well as the mind and that this necessitated some special knowledge about the intricacies of the prayer life. But King also realized that much of the language he used to define and describe prayer in the academy was off-limits in black church culture—that it was not usable in a context in which prayer, like any other spiritual matter, had always been explained not in metaphysical terms but in light of the pragmatics of human existence.[29] Even so, King discouraged any tendency to view prayer as some simplistic, incoherent liturgical language, insisting instead that prayer is sacred speech, sacred conversation, and the sacred communication of the faithful with a higher power, and also ways of thinking that inculcate certain attitudes and values in the persons who pray and that prepare them to receive God's blessings anew in their lives.[30]

King felt that his parishioners should know that the challenge of Christian discipleship begins in the heart, which, in his own mind, included prayer. Thus, the need to develop a prayer practice or habit and indeed a vibrant prayer life was axiomatic for both the pastor and the congregation. For those seeking to grow toward maturity in their faith, prayer, King held, was the source of and pathway to a grace-filled life. Moreover, he wanted the folk at Dexter, whose response to oppression was largely liturgical, to know that they always had access to the throne of grace.[31]

King's view and practice of prayer as a dimension of healing ministry also merits serious consideration. Although King, unlike pastors in the holiness and Pentecostal traditions, was not known to devote time during worship to anointing and praying for the sick and injured, he believed nonetheless that prayer embodied infinite possibilities for healing. As he saw it, his function as pastor was to lead Dexter to a fuller recognition of the healing and shaping power of prayer and to a sense of how prayer opens the faithful to the bountifulness of God's blessings.[32] This was not difficult in a culture in which church folk believed that prayer influenced God's dealings with humanity and in which a frequently heard remark was that "prayer changes things."

The idea that prayer can change the very fabric of reality permeated King's pastoral prayers, sermons, and counseling sessions at Dexter. King consistently declared that prayer was a catalyst for positive change in one's self and one's circumstances and that the promises of God are met largely through prayer. He assured his congregants that God's will and purpose were always moving in and through the prayers of the faithful and that God's powerful hand was at work in and through the dynamics of an ever-changing and unfolding universe. Consequently, they had nothing to fear from disease, misfortune, or even death.[33]

The tremendous mission potential of a praying pastor and praying congregation was most evident to King. As a pastor, he sensed the need for God not only in the lives of the folk at Dexter but also in the lives of the unchurched and in the hearts of people across the nation and world. Therefore, King's own prayers and those of his congregation were, in King's estimation, a great asset as they branched out into the mission fields in search of unsaved and lost souls. In the broadest sense, he knew that the souls of individuals, the nation, and the world were in need of redemption and transformation and that the prayers of the faithful were most relevant to this mission.[34] Interestingly enough, King was prone to highlight the significance of both a praying pastor and a praying congregation when thinking in terms of the challenges set forth in the Great Commission (Matt. 28:19-20).

The interaction between a pastor and parishioners who pray vigorously and earnestly was critical to King's definition of "the true *ekklesia*."[35] King delighted in the type of congregational setting in which the prayers of the pastor were verbally and audibly reiterated though the voices of the parishioners in a way that dismantled the traditional hierarchy of the pastor-congregation relationship in the interest of greater equality. King encouraged this type of spiritual climate at the Dexter Avenue Baptist Church. For him, collective public prayer, during which the pastor and congregation expressed themselves and their essential oneness as the body of Christ, was what made the religious pilgrimage such a life-sharing, life-giving, and life-changing experience.[36]

At the same time, King felt it necessary, as the pastor of Dexter, to warn his parishioners about approaching the activity of prayer with unrealistic expectations. The need for this kind of pastoral instruction could not have been more important, for Dexter was part of a wider church culture in which the faithful too often believed that prayer alone afforded the answer to every challenge and problem. Always mindful of this perspective, and how debilitating and disempowering it could be, King frequently addressed the need to consistently combine prayer with intelligence and responsible, positive action.[37] He wanted his people at Dexter to know that genuine prayer is never an opiate but rather a life-giving power that stimulates effort and energizes the believer for a courageous and persistent engagement with life's struggles. Furthermore, he also repeatedly reminded them that God should never be regarded as some "cosmic bell hop" to be called on for every trivial need and desire.[38]

King also desired to remove himself and his congregation as far as possible from the belief that the prayer life is an empty and meaningless function outside the Christian faith. Such a conviction was too reductionistic and exclusivistic for one who had studied different religions in seminary and graduate school and who had come to believe that there was more than one religious pathway to the deity. Convinced that God "revealed Himself to all religions" and that "there is some truth in all,"[39] King strongly rejected the thought that God hears only the cries of Christian believers. In his sermons "Worship" and "The Rewards of Worship" at Dexter, delivered in August, 1955, and April, 1957, King made special references to Islam and its tradition of "formal prayer five times a day,"[40] a practice he apparently found quite fascinating and instructive. In another sermon titled "Worship at Its Best," preached in December, 1958, King focused with telling insight on the universality of the prayer life, suggesting that he had no problem praying with Buddhists, Confucianists, Muslims, Jews, or Christians of various denominational affiliations.[41] Remarkably, the Dexter Church, with its well-educated membership, afforded the kind of atmosphere in which King could address such matters without causing a lot of confusion and conflict.

Clearly, King understood the significance of prayer in advancing understanding and mutual respect between the world's religions, but he did not speak extensively to the relevance of prayer to meaningful interreligious dialogue and cooperation. Be that as it may, King, by detecting the power and efficacy of prayer across faith traditions, distinguished himself from most pastors in the South in the 1950s. Black pastors and congregations in particular were not receptive to this outlook on any terms, and King understood this quite well. But the young pastor was too enlightened spiritually and intellectually to embrace a narrow view of God and of the scope and depth of the prayer life.[42] To be sure, King's sense of the universality or prayer and praying would prove beneficial as he sought to assert his pastoral role in the context of a freedom movement that brought together Christians, Jews, and activists who had no real devotion to formalized religion, and also as he struggled to redeem the soul of a nation and humanity as a whole.

Dexter Avenue Baptist Church was the point at which King gradually made the transition from the senior pastor of a congregation to "an American pastor,"[43] and ultimately to a pastor who longed for the redemption of the soul of humanity and of the world. King's own pastoral prayers reflect this progression; they increasingly invoke God's powerful intervention in the many problems and challenges that confronted not only the South but also the United States and the entire world. But even as King's pastoral role assumed national and international implications and significance, he felt a special need to retain some pastoral connections to a local black church. In December, 1959, King resigned from the pastorate at Dexter due to the growing demands of the civil rights movement,[44] but he then became an associate pastor with his father and brother, King Sr. and A. D. King, at the Ebenezer Baptist Church in Atlanta, his home church. This new role afforded King opportunities to continue to serve as prayer leader at various church functions, even as he fulfilled that same function as the president of the Southern Christian Leadership Conference (SCLC), a church-based civil rights organization.[45]

At Ebenezer, the traditional trajectories of Christian prayer were the norm; namely, oration, adoration, petition, intercession, and thanksgiving, with some emphasis on meditation and contemplation. Theoretically and practically, the phenomenon of prayer was linked to every existential detail in the human condition, and, aside from preaching, prayer was the most powerful element in the life of Ebenezer. But Ebenezer was not the kind of "silk-stocking church" King Jr. discovered at Dexter. Ebenezer's membership was not as class-conscious and elitist,[46] and the congregation, due

mainly to the influence of Daddy King, was more open to the traditions of the old-time Negro religion. The prayers of the deacons
during the devotional periods set the tone for worship and especially for the sermon, and Daddy King brought to his own praying
in the pulpit not only a keen sense of improvisation and spontaneity,
but a range of emotions—laughter, tears, compassionate pleading,
and wrathful condemnation—thus recalling generations of black
preachers before him.[47] Every accent, every emphasis, and every
modulation of King Sr.'s voice was always so well placed and timed
that his parishioners never ceased to be moved by his prayers. The
prayer atmosphere at Ebenezer was the major source of spiritual
sustenance for Martin Luther King Jr. in the midst of his growing
commitments and struggles as a civil rights activist and leader, and
it explained in some measure his ability to master the art of pulpit
praying and, more especially, pastoral prayer.

Despite the mounting demands of the movement, King, in
order "to be true" to his "work in the South" and his "position as
co-pastor," developed a policy of being in the pulpit at least two
Sundays a month.[48] At such times, King was expected to contribute in some way to both the prayer ministry and preaching at
Ebenezer. With the permission of Daddy King, he and his brother
A. D. sometimes alternated in offering the pastoral prayer and the
benediction, and both were known to give the invocation or to
pray over the offerings, at communion services, or during bap-
tisms. However, King seldom had time to pray with the home-
bound or hospitalized, or at funerals, weddings, Bible study, or
weekly church meetings, especially during the weekdays.

We can draw a number of conclusions regarding King's prayers
as pastor at Dexter and as copastor at Ebenezer. First, the pastoral
nature of his prayers was unmistakable. King typically prayed as
one with spiritual charge over people who had to deal daily with
pain, misfortune, self-esteem issues, sickness, and even death, and
who struggled to make sense of a capricious and at times seemingly
empty and meaningless existence. In assuring his parishioners that
God cared and answered prayer, and in highlighting prayer as a

life-giving and life-changing resource, King routinely harked back
to his own spiritual experiences to explain the reasonableness and
inevitability of prayer. Moreover, King's prayers pulsated with conviction and a caring spirit, and he exposed his own personal suf-
ferings and wounds as a virtue and as a source of healing for his
congregations.[49] The essential interdependence between the pastoral and priestly roles in King's ministry was revealed specifically
and most prominently in the ways in which he became a prayer
support for his parishioners, and in the instances in which he used
prayer as the experience through which his church folk were constantly reestablished and reaffirmed as the people of God.

A rhetorical reading of King's pastoral prayers reveals the
power of his prayer language, making it clear that his prayers were
not meaningless utterances from the heart. As a pastor, King demonstrated that prayer is in essence sacred and expressive language,[50]
and he articulated much of his vision of reconciliation and community through the power of prayer language. The prayerful quality of King's public discourse[51] is yet another illustration of how he
not only mastered the oral traditions of the black folk church and
pulpit but also achieved national and international fame with his
voice.

Of equal significance is the degree to which King's pastoral
prayers were theologically informed. For King, prayer, as pastoral conversation with God, was a theological activity, or in more
precise terms, an exercise in practical theology. In his pastoral
prayers, prayer and poetry were always intertwined with theological reflection, and one senses a vision of the kingdom of God that
embraces both every individual and the community of persons.
Furthermore, these pastoral prayers prove that King was as much
a theologian as he was a public advocate and activist,[52] a position
finding increasing support in the scholarship on this phenomenal
figure.

The prayers King offered in his service as a pastor constituted
only a part of what accounted for his significance as a theologian
and as a spiritual and moral leader. He also utilized prayer to

inspire and coalesce a movement around the ideals of freedom, justice, equal opportunity, peace, and truth. In other words, prayer and praying became for him powerful resources in the effort to transform civic and political culture and in the quest for a new nation and a new world order. This point is explored in greater depth in the next chapter.

King sitting and meditating in Birmingham City Jail, 1967.
Courtesy of Wyatt Tee Walker.

SPIRITS SOARING UPWARD | 5
PRAYER AND THE SOUNDS
OF STRUGGLE, 1955–68

We kneel, how weak! We rise, how full of power.
—Richard Chenevix Trench[1]

Pray to die to your seeing and to rise up in the seeing of thy Savior, and then thou will see the difference between God's holy will, and thy carnal will.
—Rebecca Cox Jackson[2]

Help me, O God, to see that I'm just a symbol of a movement.
—Martin Luther King Jr.[3]

Prayer helped Martin Luther King Jr. to discover the activity of God not only in his own daily life and activities but also in the needs of humanity and in the challenges of the world. He saw the many movements for freedom in his time as outpourings of God's spirit on the nation and the world, and prayer went hand in hand with his spirited call to resist systemic, social evil in all forms.[4] This view of prayer's connection to God's work in the world, perhaps more than anything else, reflected King's vital and distinctive blend of spirituality and social vision as well as his keen sense of the tremendous value and creative potential of prayer. It also explains why King made prayer central to the struggle for civil and human rights. As far as King was concerned, he was involved in essentially "a spiritual movement"[5] and not simply a struggle for equal rights, social justice, and peace; this invariably meant that prayer and praying, much like the spiritual discipline of nonviolence, had to be for him a daily activity and a total way of life. Otherwise, the quest to redeem and transform the moral and political spirit of the nation and of humanity as a whole would ultimately prove futile and perhaps even counterproductive.

King's encounters with crisis after crisis in his protest against the personal and institutional racism of white America reinforced his conception of prayer as lived experience and as part of an engaged spirituality developed in the midst of conflict and action.[6] It is often said that the movement began with a song, but in King's case it actually began with a prayer. The date was December 5, 1955; the scene was King's private study in his home at 309 South Jackson Street in Montgomery; and the challenge was a speech that he, as the newly-elected president of the Montgomery Improvement Association (MIA), the organization formed to lead the bus boycott, had to hastily prepare for the very first mass meeting held at the Holt Street Baptist Church in connection with the bus boycott. Having only fifteen minutes to prepare what he called "the most decisive speech of my life," King, "obsessed by" feelings of "inadequacy" and in "a state of anxiety," turned to that "power whose matchless strength stands over against the frailties and inadequacies of human nature." King prayed for God's guidance in delivering a speech that would be "militant enough" to arouse black people to "positive action" and "moderate enough" to keep their fervor "within controllable and Christian bounds." The speech, which called boycotters to courageous protest grounded in Christian love and democratic values, evoked more applause than any speech or sermon King had given up to that point, thus reinforcing his belief that God had the power to "transform" human weakness into a "glorious opportunity."[7] This experience confirmed King's faith in what his ancestors had long declared about the sheer discipline, immense potential, and enduring power of prayer; and it highlighted his sense of the significance of prayer as lived theology.[8]

As the pastor of the Dexter Avenue Baptist Church and a leader in the bus boycott, King increasingly came to see that secret communication with God in his private study or "closet," so to speak, was as important as praying publicly in his pulpit. Evidently, he had other private experiences during which prayer translated a paralyzing impotence into unshakable courage, frustrating uncertainty into incurable hope, and life's hardships into amazing vitality and feelings of triumph.[9] In January, 1956, as the fervor driving the Montgomery bus boycott reached fever pitch, King received a telephone call at midnight from a racist who called him a "nigger" and threatened to kill him and "blow up" his home. Deeply disturbed and unable to sleep, King retreated to his kitchen for coffee, thinking that this could possibly provide some relief. Love for family and church, devotion to the struggle, and feelings of utter helplessness gripped him in that moment of deep restlessness, painful stillness, and desperate searching. Knowing that the theology he had studied in the corridors of academia could not help him and that he had nowhere else to turn, King had a face-to-face encounter with what he, in the tradition of his forebears, called "a Waymaker," exposing his fears, insecurities, and vulnerabilities with sincerity and humility. Great comfort came as an "inner voice" spoke to King, reminding him that he was not alone, commanding him to "stand up" for righteousness, justice, and truth, and assuring him that "lo, I will be with you, even to the end of the world."[10]

This serendipitous experience further convinced King that hardship, frustration, and bewilderment are often the points at which one meets God through solitude and prayer, a notion clearly substantiated by the black experience in religion. In that moment of quiet brooding, commonly referred to as "the vision in the kitchen," King found new life in prayer, was reminded that prayer indeed mattered, and began to believe anew in how the sovereign work of the Almighty was being manifested in both his own life and in the bus protest. Moreover, the experience deepened his

sense of what it meant to follow Jesus Christ as a passionate dis-
ciple, and he came to see that prayer would be a vital dimension
of that which enabled him sufficiently to carry out his work.[11] In a
general sense, the experience in the kitchen further equipped King
to speak from experience and thus authoritatively about the saving
power of prayer. The spiritual growth wrought by that experience
would become increasingly essential in sustaining King's commitment to nonviolent struggle and in determining the nature of his
responses to crises in his life.[12]

Considering the social, economic, and political dynamics at
work in the 1950s, King was always willing and eager to assume
the role of public prayer leader. In fact, he felt that praying publicly was central to his calling as a national leader and especially
to his role as the voice of a spiritual people imbued with a messi-
anic sense of vocation and mission. He saw that public prayer, like
the singing of the spirituals and anthems of the movement, was a
powerful aspect of the spirituality that bonded his people in the
face of oppression and that gave them the will and determination
to survive, struggle, and be free, even against seemingly invincible
odds.[13] Again and again, King received practical lessons in the unifying power of public prayer from ordinary church folk who were
forced to drift in and out of the disturbed world of white racists,
who were the embodiments of lived faith, and who had literally
built churches and kept families and neighborhoods together by
"talking to de Lawd" and making painful sacrifices.[14]

King's role as public prayer leader extended into his activities as both a pastor and civil rights leader. Much like the worship
experience at the Dexter Avenue Baptist Church, the board meetings of the MIA always included prayers, songs, scripture readings,
and speeches, all of which reflected a nonviolent tone, and King,
as the organization's chairman, often gave the opening or closing
prayer. At times, MIA board members such as Willie F. Alford,
Ralph W. Hilson, G. Franklin Lewis, and B. D. Lambert, all clergymen, were asked to offer the invocation and prayer as part of the
benediction.[15] King constantly highlighted the need to remain in a

prayerful mood considering the challenges his people faced daily, and he insisted that MIA decisions regarding the boycott be carefully "thought about" and "prayed over" before being implemented through practical action.[16]

Earnest and fervent prayer was expected of all MIA board members, clergy and laity, and King was frequently moved by the content and tone of the prayers he heard, but there were occasionally comical sides and shades to the activities as they unfolded at board meetings. At one particular MIA board meeting, the Reverend B. D. Lambert gave a "shouting presentation" that flowed into a kind of "singing prayer," and Lambert's whooping made King uncomfortable, uneasy, and restless, especially in view of the setting. Another MIA member observed King "crossing and uncrossing his legs" and "placing first one and then the other hand over his face," and it seemed that King literally struggled "to prevent his smiles from leading to open laughter." King is said to have given the appearance of "definite relief once the prayer had ended."[17]

The highly emotionally charged prayers were more acceptable to King when they were uttered in more public settings, such as during church services and at mass meetings, where large numbers of church folk were present. In such settings, prayer always included an impassioned call to struggle, and King and other clergymen did most of the praying. The dynamic prayers they recited often took on the flavor of folk sermons and songs, as audiences responded with shouts of "Please, hear our feeble cry," "Be with us, Lord," and "We can't make it without Thee." Even Robert S. Graetz, one of the very few white ministers involved in the Montgomery protest, was moved profoundly when occasionally praying at mass meetings. At one such meeting, Graetz offered a stirring prayer, asking God for strength in the face of the rising tide of evil, as he, King, and Ralph D. Abernathy, with eyes closed and hands raised, stood on the platform at one of the black churches in Montgomery.[18] The impact of such moments of desperation and prayer were captured in King's sermons and writings for that period.

King himself occasionally became quite emotional while praying at mass meetings, especially after protesters were attacked and homes and churches bombed by white bigots. "Discouraged" and "revolted by the bombings," and feeling "a personal sense of guilt" for all these problems, King was on one occasion close to tears as he asked the audience to join him in prayer. While "asking God's guidance and direction," King was caught in "the grip of an emotion" he "could not control" and actually "broke down in public." His prayer built to an exuberant sung finale, with the audience crying out and rejoicing. "So intense was the reaction" that King could not finish his prayer. With the help of fellow ministers, who put their arms around him, King was slowly lowered to his seat.[19]

Here was an occasion when the traditional prayer meeting served to solidify a despised and abused people around a common faith, hope, purpose, and strategy for change. Though caught in the web of guilt and emotion, King did not stand alone, for the sense of being both a suffering community and a divinely ordained instrument for much-needed social change proved overwhelming for all who participated. The emotive qualities of the black church, which often exploded into handclapping and joyous shouts, and which King had frowned on as a boy, took on a new and more personal dimension for the civil rights leader. Prayer rose to sermon, tears gave way to rejoicing, and King's calm manner surrendered to an infectious frenzy.[20] Hence, King's connection to the ecstatic side of the black prayer tradition and to the African American worship experience as a whole became amazingly real. Clearly, scholars must take this and other of King's experiences concerning public prayer in the civil rights crusade more seriously if they are to bring a true sense of the richness and power of the black church experience to the daunting work of King interpretation.

King's emerging significance as public prayer leader in the context of a social movement requires some attention to what he actually prayed for during those years in Montgomery. This is not merely some curious or trivial concern, for it goes to the matter of King's spirituality and worldview. King believed that the more praying there was on the part of committed persons, the stronger the force against evil and the greater the opportunities for creating a better society and world. Thus, he prayed for the strength and continuing efforts of all persons of goodwill; for the oppressed and exploited worldwide; for leaders who acted out of conscience, integrity, and a deep spirit of commitment; for God's help in working through problems "gigantic in scope and chaotic in detail"; for the elimination of "self-defeating" hatred and methods of violence; and for the creation of the beloved community and "a new world."[21]

Convinced that genuine praying stimulated desire and effort and inspired activity, King buttressed his active role in the Montgomery bus protest by daily prayer.[22] He constantly asked God to help him understand that he was a product of "the zeitgeist," or spirit of the times, to keep his own leadership in "true perspective," to see that he was merely "a symbol" of the movement and not the movement itself, and to know that he was where he was because of "the forces of history" and the fifty thousand Negroes in Montgomery who supported and walked the streets with him.[23] King also prayed that the leadership of the Negro people would remain wise, steadfast, and courageous in its pursuit of "the great city of integration"; that it would "avoid the extremes of hotheadedness and Uncle Tomism"; that "the white moderates of the South" would "rise up" courageously and assume some leadership role "in this period of tense transition"; and that ministers, lay leaders, businesspersons, and professional people would employ their "talents" and "finances" to "lead the people" toward "the promised land of freedom" through "nonviolent means."[24]

The black community of Montgomery as a whole was always uppermost in King's thinking when he prayed. He asked God to take away the fear that shackled too many of his people; to remove all bitterness from their hearts; to help them accept themselves and to make proper use of the tools they had; and to give them the strength of mind, spirit, and body to face "the realities of life" and "to keep walking for freedom."[25] This type of unselfish praying, or praying that was other-directed rather than self-centered, helped establish King's prominence as both a spiritual leader and moral crusader among his people.

King frequently challenged his fellow activists regarding the need to pray diligently, sincerely, and unceasingly for the success of the movement and the elimination of "the evils that still beset our nation." His calls to prayer were probably heard most often within the circle of activists that constituted the MIA and later his Southern Christian Leadership Conference (SCLC), which was a South-wide organization founded in 1957 to coordinate local protest activities and to bring Christian discipline to the movement.[26] King assured his fellow activists that God heard them and answered their prayers, a point made emphatically in his "Call to a Prayer Pilgrimage for Freedom" in April, 1957, during which he likened all freedom fighters to the founding fathers, who prayed for wisdom and strength "in the wilderness of a new land"; to the slaves and their offspring, who prayed for "emancipation and human dignity"; and to people of color everywhere who sought divine guidance in times of crisis.[27] Drawing on the story of Jesus in the Garden of Gethsemane, King reminded fellow activists that the movement was actually "a bitter cup" that freedom fighters had to drink daily, and that they, like Jesus, had to sometimes pray, "Let this cup pass from me," while also remaining willing and able to make the transition to "nevertheless, not my will, but Thy will be done" (Matt. 26:39).[28] In other words, the idea of prayer as an escape from the cup, or from the will to act on principle for the common good, should never be considered.[29] Movement for King meant combining prayer with an activist ethic.

Through letters, telephone calls, and other means, King sent out prayer requests on behalf of the movement in Montgomery. Such efforts, in conjunction with his participation in prayer meetings, prayer vigils, and prayer pilgrimages,[30] were designed to forge a unity of minds, hearts, and spirits in the midst of the larger struggle to transform unjust laws, systems, institutions, and practices. Prayer and protest went hand in hand, as people from different church and denominational backgrounds took to the streets and made their case for a more just, peaceful, and inclusive society.[31] Thus, the claim that "Black folk basically preached, prayed, and sang their way through the bus boycott and the movement"[32] is easy to sustain by any standard.

A study of certain secondary sources yields some interesting observations regarding the role and significance of prayer for King and the larger black community in Montgomery. We have already mentioned Mervyn A. Warren's references to the importance of "preparatory prayer" and the "prayer of relinquishment" in helping King meet the many challenges in Montgomery.[33] Harold A. Carter makes some equally interesting and provocative remarks about "the prayer tradition of black people," asserting that "throughout the Montgomery bus boycott, Black prayers were used for inner release of potentially violent reactions, while sustaining some sense of direction toward freedom and the beloved community for all men."[34] Carter maintains that King taught the people of Montgomery that the weapon of prayer was ultimately more powerful and effective than any gun or bomb, a message they, due to "a deep tradition of Christian stoicism," listened to and responded to quite well:

> Dr. King used this long prayer tradition to teach Black people that the one who faces life with a prayer is not weak. On the contrary, he is exhibiting far more strength than the one supplied with man-made forces. He taught that soul power was far more effective in human redemption than physical power. . . . No one in modern times has lifted the dimension of facing life on one's knees as has the late Dr. Martin Luther King, Jr. When he called on his followers to face their enemies with a prayer and non-violence based in Christian love, he was speaking to a people whose history made them receptive to this message. Waging war on one's knees was not new! Dr. King simply gave it a new dimension. . . . The results of this teaching found many Black persons ready and willing to take the teaching of facing life on

one's knees and using it to bring freedom from unjust social laws, unjust political laws, while generating a healthier sense of community among Black people particularly and among all who shared this philosophy generally. This was the teaching that undergirded the civil rights movement under the leadership of Dr. King.[35]

Carter elaborates on the point regarding the black prayer tradition in more revealing terms, focusing especially on the galvanizing power of both prayer and the singing of the spirituals:

> In Montgomery, Alabama, the traditional prayer meeting served to bring together an oppressed people under a bold new philosophy, nonviolence based on Christian love. The songs of slavery came alive, matched with the thrust of spontaneous prayers for enemies and for freedom. Suddenly people of all colors and creeds began to take notice, as the prayers of former slave children were ringing out from jails, courthouses, streets, and churches.[36]

Carter rightly contends that the "Black prayer tradition, so effectively used in the Montgomery bus boycott, was the rallying point for ministers and Christian laymen during later struggles for freedom in Albany, Birmingham, Selma, and Washington, D.C."[37] The prayer vigil was carried over, perhaps to a greater degree, from Montgomery to Albany, Georgia, the focal point of King's second major attempt at social protest. In mid-1961 in Albany, King and Ralph D. Abernathy, chief consultants to the Albany Movement, issued a statement, "Why Our Prayer Vigil," as a reaction to the failure of city officials to meet and engage in good-faith negotiations with them. This planned "vigil of prayer" was designed to help soften the hearts of police chief Laurie Pritchett and other white city officials, thus preparing them to "sit with us at the conference table" and make some "justifiable resolutions of our legitimate grievances" concerning the entire system of segregation in

Albany.[38] In his "Message from Jail" (1962) in Albany, King also raised the possibility of "prayer marches"[39] as a rallying point for a more radical challenge to injustice and the stubbornness of the governing elite in Albany.

King invited seventy-five Protestants, Catholics, and Jews, all ministers, priests, and rabbis, to join what was essentially an across-the-board, full-scale assault on segregation in Albany. The group was summoned to Atlanta "to support a prayer vigil for racial justice in Albany."[40] For King, the power and potential of prayer in the context of this ecumenical crusade against injustice could not have been more evident. The prayer vigil painfully revealed a powerful undercurrent of dissatisfaction with the status quo, offering practical lessons in both engaged spirituality and participatory democracy.

Hundreds of clergy and laity were jailed in Albany and surrounding towns, but they, under King's leadership and inspiration, turned their jail cells into settings for prayer meetings and the singing of freedom songs, thus recalling Paul and Silas's experience in prison (Acts 16:16-38). King never forgot those times, when prayer and song released him and other blacks in jail from sadness and solemnity into joy and celebration. King also learned and benefited spiritually and otherwise from the praying and singing that filled the air in churches, that pervaded the atmosphere during kneel-ins on the steps at city hall, and that occurred everywhere else he gathered with his aides and other blacks.[41] Art and the struggle for freedom found a pleasant mixture, despite the verbal abuses and the unspeakable acts of violence visited on King and other peaceful protesters by white law enforcement officials.

This was also the case in 1963, with SCLC's Project Confrontation in Birmingham, which targeted the business community, separate lunch counters, and discriminatory hiring practices. Movement prayers, freedom songs, and the pledge to the nonviolent crusade were inseparable for King. He eagerly participated in prayer meetings, prayer vigils, and kneel-in campaigns, and he united forces with ministers, priests, and rabbis "around the old-time freedom prayers and the Black spiritual."[42] His decision to disobey or defy unjust laws and court injunctions was preceded by periods of both private and public prayer, during which he asked God for strength, direction, and companionship. King and the other marchers left black churches "inspired by a continuous flow of song and prayer before facing Bull Connor and his ruthless police dogs," powerful water hoses, and electrifying cattle prods; and "whenever persons were arrested for breaking unjust laws, traditional black prayers were supporting their efforts."[43]

King was also known to steep himself in the quiet character of prayer and meditation while in Birmingham. While sitting in the Birmingham City Jail, he was given to silent prayer, meditation, and periods of serious thought and reflection. The celebrated "Letter from the Birmingham City Jail" (1963) grew largely out of those moments of secret communication with God. At times, King rented a hotel room and retreated to it for a prayer-centered day, or "a day of silence," during which he, alone and burdened by the weight or enormous responsibilities, poured his heart out to God.[44] This personal prayer retreat was essential for stress relief and anxiety reduction, but it was significant in other ways for King. It afforded opportunities for him to create sacred space and time to develop a thriving inner spiritual life in the context of struggle, and this could not have been more essential for one who had such a deep appreciation of the potential of the Christian inner life. Because King was on a mission ordained by God, he had personal devotional needs, and spiritual renewal through inner silence and contemplative prayer became a significant part of his practice of faith. King needed these times for strength and courage; to endure ridicule, scorn, and threats against his life; and for the kind of wisdom and attitudinal posture required to keep moving forward. Through these times, he came to know the deep joy, peace, and sense of relief that come only through praying alone and in secrecy.[45]

King's spirituality actually called for a wedding of prayerful discernment and loving activity. This too helps explain his emphasis on prayer as silent language and as quiet contemplation and meditation. For King, an expression of the inner self, or prayer as an inner quieting of the spirit, translated into more competent and effective leadership in the struggle for freedom, justice, and human dignity. By balancing silent prayer, contemplation, and meditation with organized and sustained activism in the public sphere, he forged a unique model of spirituality. In other words, King's habit of praying in silence stimulated his own personal transformation in the context of a larger quest for social transformation.[46]

In Birmingham, King turned to prayer as a source of empowerment and reaffirmation, especially when black people were physically attacked and churches and homes were burned or bombed. The bombing of the Sixteenth Street Baptist Church, the headquarters for SCLC's Project Confrontation, in September, 1963, was one case in point. Four little girls died, and King prayed and spoke words of comfort in an effort to rekindle the spirits of people who were stricken with grief and who would have otherwise lost faith in God's presence and love. Here King's image as "the high priest" of the movement[47] was legitimized. His "Eulogy for the Martyred Children" (1963), which is peppered with prayerful reflections and assurances of God's love and activity in history, became the experience through which the community reestablished and reaffirmed itself as the people of God and as cosufferers with God for the improvement of the human condition.[48] King was compelled once again to contemplate the possibilities of prayer in times of sorrow, suffering, and death.

King's "I Have a Dream" speech, delivered at the march on Washington in August, 1963, was part of God's answer to centuries of black prayers. Harold A. Carter is right in saying that King's "dream of true brotherhood, respect for human dignity, and the essential worth of all God's people, provided the Black prayer tradition one of its finest hours."[49] During the planning stage for the event, King prayed for its success and enduring, positive impact on the United States, and he urged ministers and churches throughout the country to hold local prayer vigils in support of the civil rights cause and agenda. Washington, D.C., as the nation's capital, had long held a particular significance for King as the context for massive prayer pilgrimages, especially after the prayer pilgrimage in May, 1957,[50] and it was only natural for him to stress prayer as an essential component of the great march. This was all the more important since the march on Washington was designed to dramatize the problems of bigotry, intolerance, and injustice before a nation that claimed to be grounded in Judeo-Christian values. The enthusiastic involvement of Protestants, Jews, and Catholics in the march must have reinforced King's sense of what can be accomplished when people of different religions pray, sing, and struggle together.[51]

As much as any King-led civil rights campaigns, the struggles in St. Augustine, Florida, and Selma, Alabama, revealed the cultural, spiritual, and artistic links between prayer, music, and movement. In St. Augustine in 1964, King continued to combine an active personal prayer life with a heavy involvement in the type of participatory praying and singing for which southern black churches were widely known. The images of church deacons crying out to God on their knees during devotional periods, of protesters swaying to and fro while chanting and singing freedom songs, and of speeches rising to the dizzy heights of emotion always moved and reinvigorated King. The complete breakdown of law and order in St. Augustine, as symbolized by the menacing white mobs that verbally insulted and physically attacked blacks, made the experience of prayer and praying all the more necessary for him,[52] and quite comforting and enriching for the souls of all who struggled daily.

During the voting rights campaign in Selma in 1965, King and other activists creatively drew on the spiritual disciplines of black churches, uniting the prayer circle and the picket line. The experience gave a new image to public and communal prayer. As the demonstrators prepared for the great march from Selma to Montgomery, the media captured King and other ministers in a circle on their knees, with Ralph Abernathy, King's closest associate, praying that blacks and whites would learn to live together in peace. The stage had already been set at the Brown Chapel African Methodist Episcopal Church (AME), with the singing of spirituals like "Joshua Fit the Battle of Jericho" and "Ain't Gonna Let Nobody Turn Me Round," which created a medley of sounds punctuating the prayers offered by clergy.[53] In any case, Abernathy's circle prayer, offered in the presence of policemen wearing helmets and holding clubs, really highlighted the power of the black prayer experience as a weapon against oppression. It also revealed much about the kind of creative spiritual genius that fueled the movement as a whole.

The Selma campaign proved significant for King's role as a public prayer leader, in part because of the murder of Jimmie Lee Jackson, the Reverend James Reeb, and Viola Liuzzo. In the midst of these tragedies, King remained in a prayerful spirit despite his and others' occasional expressions of anger and outrage. With his right hand raised and surrounded by other ministers, he recited a prayer at the grave of Jackson in Marion, Alabama, in March, 1965, as others prayed silently around and about him. King's eulogy at Reeb's memorial service effectively amounted to an exercise in prayerful preaching, and he responded to Liuzzo's murder with calls for prayer, sympathy, and rational action.[54] Once again, King's role as high priest of the movement reemerged in all of its dynamism and style. He resorted to prayer as a way of mediating between the living and the dead in order to ease the pain and lessen the hardship of the living, particularly in a society in which people could be so brutally killed for merely standing up for what was right and just.[55]

The importance of King's role as public prayer leader in Selma owed much to the ecumenical character of the campaign. Four hundred white ministers comprising Protestants, Catholics, and Jews went to Selma and, due largely to King's leadership and inspiration, were exposed to the essentials of the black prayer tradition and the black worship experience as a whole. Most of these religious leaders had never had such an experience, especially in the black church in the South. King saw in this checkered mix of religious personalities a real testimony to the power of both prayer and careful planning and organization, and he, preparing to lead thousands "through a wilderness of State Troopers," prayed that the unity and rare comradeship displayed there would also become characteristic of the South and indeed the entire country.[56] It was a prayer for the ultimate actualization of the beloved community, and as such it could not have been more appropriate for the occasion.

When King and his SCLC staff were invited to participate in the Chicago Freedom Movement in 1965, they took with them the spiritual resources of the southern black church. King brought those resources to bear not only on his efforts to end slum conditions but also on his function as public prayer leader. In 1965–66, he prayed in a number of black churches in Chicago and used prayer as a means of uniting blacks and sympathetic whites in a struggle to eliminate indecent housing and unfair real estate practices. In the late afternoon of July 26, 1965, King, standing on "a truck bed in the presence of 30,000 marchers and hundreds of others who listened from office building windows," recited a stirring prayer, asking God to bless the city "set so impressively by the majestic waters of Lake Michigan."[57] King also prayed for relief from the "deplorable conditions" in housing, schools, and employment in Chicago; for guidance in overcoming its subtle and blatant patterns of racial discrimination; for political leadership that would value and meet the needs of all Chicagoans; and for a new "city of brotherhood where success is founded upon service."[58] Interestingly enough, King's prayer for Chicago reflected his growing concern for economic justice issues.

During the last three years of his life, King seemed more intentional about approaching both life and the movement prayerfully. This growing spirit most likely resulted from the increased threats against his life and the heightened expectation that he would be the victim of an assassin's bullet. As Harold A. Carter has indicated, King made prayer "an integral part of every struggle, meeting, and decision."[59] He prayed, secretly and publicly, as he marched with sanitation workers in Memphis, as he planned the Poor People's Campaign, as he cried out against America's misadventure in Vietnam, and as he called for the triumph of a spirit of international peace.[60] But King's hopes were often frustrated, and his moods became increasingly bleak, especially after the very last demonstration he led was marred by violence in Memphis. Television cameras captured King in Memphis only days before his death, singing with folded arms in a circle with other ministers, with his eyes fixed upward toward the heavens. King sensed that his days were numbered, and he could see that the influence he once had was eroding under the challenge of more militant forces within the freedom movement and in the face of a federal government that seemed determined to isolate and ultimately silence him. But he also understood that God, his cosmic companion, was still standing with him, even in his darkest hour.[61] It must have occurred to King in those final days that prayer was the only power he could wholeheartedly believe in and rely on.

Generally speaking, we can and should make a number of observations about King's movement prayers and about how he viewed and practiced praying in relationship to the struggle for freedom, justice, equal opportunity, and peace. In a very real sense, prayer became a part of King's search for more authentic paths to the fulfillment of Christian social responsibility. This is why, in the context of the movement, he experimented with prayer in different forms and settings, emphasizing particularly the importance and effectiveness of "the call to prayer," "prayer meetings," "prayer pilgrimages," "prayer vigils," "prayer rallies," "prayer marches," "the prayer circle," and "services of prayer and thanksgiving."[62] Praying in the streets became as necessary for King as his sermons in churches and his exhortations at mass meetings, especially in view of the evolving social, political, and economic dynamics of his times.

Prayer was actually a part of the religiously informed conscience that King brought to the freedom struggle, and his movement prayers reflected his conviction that prayer is an essential ingredient in any social movement truly rooted in spiritual and moral values. In King's estimation, the civil rights movement made this evident. He prayed for a true Christian solution to the heart-breaking and mind-boggling problems of racial oppression, economic exploitation, and violence and human destruction, and saw prayer as an aspect of the process leading from "self-purification" to "a disciplined course of action."[63] Convinced that there is no substitute for prayer in any Christian social movement, he never relegated prayer to a secondary force in the struggle. For King, the prayer circle, prayer vigils, and other forms of prayer were as vital to the success of the movement as the picket lines, the sit-ins, the freedom rides, and the marches. As the leader of a movement, King held that the experience of entering God's presence through prayer was absolutely indispensable, and he always approached social activism with a prayerful attitude.[64]

King habitually entered the field of prayer with probing questions about how he might best effect change in his own world and in the larger world of injustice. Self-centered prayer was never a spiritual option for him; it violated both his sense of communal ethics and his total life commitment to worldwide social justice. In King's mind, the continuum of prayer never simply extended from the self to God, with no reference to others. In a creative and altruistic sense, prayer for him involved transforming oneself as well as healing and empowering others, and prayer compelled him to take his share in the plan of a God who so loved the world that this God sacrificed all for its redemption. In other words, prayer heightened King's passion for human beings and reinforced his determination to struggle for the highest moral and ethical ideal, even at the risk of life itself.[65] Convinced that prayer could sometimes achieve what could not be accomplished through nonviolent direct action and acts of civil disobedience, King constantly prayed in churches, in his study, in jail cells, in the streets, and in hotel rooms, always casting a hopeful eye toward possibilities for greater strides toward freedom. Whatever mistakes King made, and there were many in his private and public lives, they were not due to the poverty of his own prayer life or to an understanding of prayer that alienates one from humanity and the world.

Prayer was King's secret weapon in the civil rights movement. In no uncertain terms, he affirmed both openly and in subtle ways the indispensable relationship between the activity of praying and the quest for greater rights and freedom. When movement leaders were cursed, arrested, assaulted, or killed in street demonstrations, King and others found the will to go on through prayer. King really believed that under the power of prayer, no force of evil, however great and menacing, could destroy the forward march toward freedom, justice, and peace. This incurable optimism and hope that King brought to the movement stemmed first and foremost from his unwavering faith in the power and efficacy of prayer, for he knew of instances in history in which sincere praying culminated in acts of defiance, resistance to both personal and social evils, and the replacement of an old order with a new order.[66]

King's movement prayers reveal much about his self-understanding as preacher, pastor, and priest, but they are just as useful for analyzing his prophetic concerns. The prayers could be labeled prophetic for a couple of reasons. First, King turned his prayers inward, to keep himself true to his calling and mission. He knew that he too was under the judgment of everything he proclaimed and did, and he never had any problem commending himself to God's care, asking God to teach him and show him God's will and purpose for himself and the people he represented. In short, King's movement prayers stand as living proof that he understood, despite his growing fame and influence, that the ultimate power was not himself, but God.[67] Second, King's prayers were in essence a warning signal to his people, the nation, and indeed the entire world that God would not long tolerate idolatry and the mistreatment and exploitation of the poor and weak by the privileged, and that humanity should repent, seek God, avoid evil, and act justly in the face of the coming judgment.[68] In his capacity as the leader of a movement, King actually elevated prayer to the pinnacle of personal and prophetic witness.

The possibilities of prayer eased any doubts King may have had about the realization of the beloved community in history.

This helps explain King's ability to make some sense of, and to live out, the dilemmas of race in his surroundings. He believed that prayer remained an indispensable means of achieving the beloved community or what he, in theological terms, called the kingdom of God on earth.[69] Here King was not being spiritually and politically naïve, for he had repeatedly experienced the effectiveness of prayer as both a cementing force and a reservoir of creative vitality in the context of the movement.

King held that there were some causal connections between prayer and the successful outcome of civil rights campaigns. This is evident from a close reading of some of his movement prayers.[70] King witnessed answers to his prayers daily as his people found unity and common ground in the struggle, as the hearts of white bigots were changed, as increasing numbers of white moderates in the South joined the civil rights program, and as barriers to equal opportunity were gradually struck down. Moreover, he saw that prayer was a wellspring of energy and inspiration for the movement, and he understood that he was effective as a civil rights activist and advocate for world peace because prayer anchored his own practical and engaged spirituality.[71] This is why King could quote his slave forebears with such confidence and enthusiasm: "Lord, we ain't what we want to be; we ain't what we ought to be; we ain't what we gonna be, but thank God, we ain't what we was."[72]

Of equal significance was King's unwavering belief in the world-transforming power of prayer. He felt that the global community could benefit immensely from the spiritual energy, courage, and sense of certainty that came through prayer, especially when prayer was offered out of a genuine respect for and affirmation of what the many church and religious traditions worldwide had to contribute to the exercise of prayer.[73] Furthermore, King had every confidence that his prayers would make a difference to the world through the God who becomes a coworker and cosufferer with humanity in the struggle to redeem and transform the human situation.[74] The illimitable resources and possibilities of prayer for him inhered in God's readiness and willingness to answer those who prayed sincerely, and who combined an active prayer life with constructive and productive strategies for destroying systems of oppression and victimization.[75]

But King was equally emphatic in insisting that prayer always be placed in practical perspective. He approached prayer as a Christian realist, knowing that misguided, abused, or misused prayer could be as ineffective as human resources in supplying the heart's desires and in vanquishing evil. Prayer for King was never an escape or a safety valve from suffering, anxiety, and danger; and he consistently warned against the misguided idea that God can do everything for humanity and that all his people had to do was pray and depend on God to correct the evils that haunted them daily. As King put it, any people struggling for a just society had also to use their minds and bodies, working vigorously to achieve their desired goals.[76] Prayer in this case, he maintained, becomes "a marvelous and necessary supplement" to human efforts. Drawing on the Exodus accounts in the Old Testament, which "functioned as an archetypical myth for the slaves"[77] and their descendants, King engaged in a spirited defense of prayer while also highlighting the significance of human initiative. He often reminded those who gathered in churches and on the streets that when Moses was leading the Israelites to the promised land, it was clear that God would not do for them what they were capable of doing for themselves.[78]

In criticizing those who resorted to prayer as an escape from responsibility and action, King occasionally alluded to Marxist dogma, which characterized religion as "the opiate of the people."[79] "As a minister," he declared, "I take prayer too seriously to use it as an excuse for avoiding work and responsibility."[80] The formula King recommended for overcoming what he labeled "the giant triplets" or "the evil triumvirate," namely, racism, poverty, and war, was the combination of prayer, intelligence, and sustained activism.[81]

Needless to say, King functioned in a culture that did not share his understanding of the role of prayer in social movements. In the presence of militants who raised the paradox of praying to a

Christian God who had long seemed oblivious to the black struggle and demands for change, he patiently affirmed and reaffirmed the need for his people to remain steadfast in the faith.[82] Perhaps more challenging for King were those seemingly well-meaning Christians who limited God's call to faithful living to prayer, meditation, and other acts of personal piety and private devotion, who acted as if prayer was only a worship resource, and who too often reduced prayer to a mere movement of the lips, an expression of empty words and thoughts, a recitation of trivial requests, a way of manipulating a higher power, or a way of groveling in the presence of a God who is more "an omnipotent czar" and "cosmic tyrant" than a loving and merciful companion.[83] Sensing this to be the case with all too many among the oppressed, King urged his people to always keep prayer in proper perspective without losing sight of both its practical limitations and endless possibilities.

King actually revitalized and enlarged the black prayer tradition as he employed it in the most important struggle for civil rights in the nation's history. As Harold A. Carter observes, "The liberating relevance of the Black prayer tradition reached its modern-day summit in the heroic life and philosophy of Martin Luther King, Jr."[84] Faced with the enormous challenge of social evil in so many shades, King, like so many of his ancestors, cabled himself to prayer. He never wavered in his conviction that prayer and action for justice are always interconnected in the Christian faith, as well as in other faith traditions. King prayed and marched with those who were poor, despised, rejected, marginalized, and abused. His sense of prayer grew out of a sensitized awareness of the plight of what he called *the least of these*[85]—those who stood at the margins of society—and prayer inspired him to act in ways that brought public-policy initiatives and systematic change on behalf of those who suffered on grounds of race and economics.

Beyond these considerations, King was inspired by the amazing possibilities that the discipline and activity of prayer afforded for growth in the spiritual lives of individuals. Thus, he wished and called for a nation that would freely and enthusiastically open itself to the timeless, limitless, and exhaustless resources of prayer. Prayer for King was food for not just the souls of individuals but for the soul of a nation that was, due to its preoccupation with power, war, and materialism, rapidly approaching what he termed "spiritual disillusionment" and "spiritual death."[86] Significantly, King's effort "to redeem the soul of America"[87] had perhaps as much to do with prayer as it did with the disciplines of creative nonviolent dissent and protest.

King's life was highly charged with the creative energy of what he called "divine companionship," "cosmic companionship," or communion with the personal God of love and reason.[88] This was clear up to that very last night in Memphis, April 3, 1968, when King stood in the Mason Temple Church, closed his eyes, and prayed silently before telling the world about his mountaintop experience and his vision of the promised land. The next day he succumbed to an assassin's bullet.

The vision, power, and genius King brought to the civil rights cause were nurtured in prayer. Consequently, he taught this country and the world something quite profound about the meaningful prayer life, and about the type of spiritual qualities needed to cultivate and sustain a complete and productive life more generally. King also showed humanity, through his words and most certainly his deeds, that the true test of a genuine work of God is always the pervasiveness of the spirit of prayer. This part of King's legacy, though too often ignored, remains vital and relevant today, and it suggests possibilities for forging creative and inseparable links between personal spirituality and social transformation. This will be further highlighted in the next chapter, the last in this volume.

Two young boys pray at the King gravesite after September 11, 2001.
Source: Thomson Reuters.

TOWARD A
HARMONIOUS WHOLE

PRAYER AND PRAYING IN THE SPIRIT OF KING

|6

They who have steeped their souls in prayer
can every anguish calmly bear.
—Richard M. Milnes[1]

Martin Luther King spoke with the tongues of men and of angels.
—L. Harold DeWolf [2]

I believe that there is a personal power in this universe that works to bring
the disconnected assets of reality into a harmonious whole.
—Martin Luther King Jr.[3]

Martin Luther King Jr. is honored by people of faith worldwide as a paragon of godly devotion and as the beacon of an all-engaging and practical spirituality. His untimely death, on April 4, 1968, brought tributes from every corner of the globe, and many prayed for his soul and for the realization of his dream. Pope Paul VI prayed that "the virtues of justice and international love, for which Dr. King stood," would "come to be respected everywhere."[4] Jacqueline Kennedy, the widow of the late President John F. Kennedy, said of King: "I pray that with the price he paid—his life—he will make room in people's hearts for love, not hate."[5] Since that sad day, interfaith prayer meetings, prayer breakfasts, and prayer vigils and marches are among the range of activities held each year in King's memory. King is celebrated in this manner not only for his social activism and outstanding contributions to the civil and human rights causes, but also because his deep faith and prophetic wisdom penetrated so deeply into the fabric of human affairs.[6] This is most evident from the foregoing discussion of King as a public prayer leader and as one who combined an energetic prayer life and ministry with a profound social vision.

The Martin Luther King Jr. Center for Nonviolent Social Change, located in Atlanta, Georgia, surrounded by King's birthplace, the Ebenezer Baptist Church, and King's gravesite, has become a Mecca for millions who wish to honor King through prayers and other acts of faith. Thousands make what is essentially a pilgrimage to the center each year, bowing and kneeling at King's gravesite, at his birthplace, at Ebenezer Church, or in the interfaith chapel. Silent and public acts of prayer and meditation occur regularly on the grounds of the center.[7] At public gatherings, the sounds and rhythms of prayer are almost always punctuated by the quiet roar of vehicles passing slowly by, but the sacredness of the occasion is never disturbed nor compromised.

But questions arise in any serious discussion of the meaningfulness and relevance of King today for those who wish to develop a stronger life of prayer or delve more deeply into the practice of centering prayer. What significance could King's prayer life and philosophy of prayer possibly have in a world in which there is such a plurality of religious and secular worldviews, and in which the terrain of religion and spirituality has so rapidly shifted since his death? Is prayer rendered meaningless by the advance of information technology and human knowledge? If spiritual malnourishment is the great tragedy of this age, as many leading religious figures declare, then what can we gain from a spiritual journey with King through prayer? Is King useful in reviving the prayerful experiences needed to overcome much of the spiritual malaise in our society and world?[8] These questions form the basis of the discussion that follows.

These are times in which the importance of and need for prayer are highlighted in many ways in religious settings and in the broader public square. Interfaith national day of prayer gatherings and prayer surges for peace have become perhaps more common today than in King's times. People in cities throughout the United States participate each year in a national day of prayer, with worship services, musical performances, prayer rallies, moments of silence, and other "prayer-focused events."[9] Under the administration of Barack Obama, prayer has become more common at presidential appearances, "including at nonreligious events such as stimulus rallies."[10] In May, 2009, President Obama signed an official proclamation in recognition of the national day of prayer, and he actually attended the fifty-fourth annual national prayer breakfast.[11] Also, prayer at sports events at all levels in this country, from grade school to the professional ranks, has become more of a fixture in the culture.[12] Some churches are even promoting the idea of a world day of prayer.[13] All of these activities stem from the conviction, expressed by King as early as the 1950s, that prayer should always be an indispensable supplement to human initiatives.[14]

King believed and often said that problems and challenges have a way of forcing people to face life on their knees with their heads bowed,[15] and this is most certainly the case in the contemporary age. The tremendous emphasis on prayer and praying owes much to the sense of uncertainty and insecurity people feel in an increasingly globalized world, which is becoming more hostile, complex, and capricious. During the current tough and challenging economic downturn, people of faith are increasingly calling on a high power to bless corporate executives, the companies over which they preside, and their pools of employees.[16] Prayer centers are receiving millions of requests annually from people who are facing financial difficulties and seeking employment.[17] Prayers are being offered in a struggle to deal with mounting cycles of criminal violence; and natural disasters such as tornadoes, hurricanes, and the recent earthquakes in Abruzzo, Italy, and Haiti, during which thousands died.[18] National prayer days are literally saturated with

prayers offered on behalf of soldiers at war abroad, and men are
seen praying in the streets of Baghdad for peace and security after
the withdrawal of U.S. troops.[19] The belief that prayer and meditation can ease stress and anxiety in troubled times is as pervasive
as it was in the days of King,[20] but few are as intentional as King
was about combining fervent and earnest prayer with sustained
activism against the institutions and structures responsible for so
much of the economic exploitation and the violence and human
destruction.

Perhaps more than in King's times, the role of prayer in public
life and in the shaping of public policy initiatives is being debated
widely today. One of the most controversial issues in 1964 was "the
question of school prayer," which was ruled unconstitutional by
the Supreme Court. King supported the high court's decision over
against Alabama Governor George C. Wallace and other political conservatives whom he called "the Radical Right," arguing that
in "a pluralistic society such as ours," no one could legitimately
"determine what prayer shall be spoken, and by whom."[21] The
school prayer issue is still dividing Americans at all levels, thus
suggesting the timelessness of certain concerns that King raised.
Many on the so-called Left contend that school prayer transgresses
church-state boundaries and violates the U.S. constitution's religion clauses, while those on the religious and political Right take
the opposite position.[22] King, who found something positive even
in the claims of atheists,[23] would undoubtedly take sides with left-
wing liberals today, in part out of respect for religious pluralism
and also because of Constitutional concerns. He strongly criticized
right-wingers in his day for supporting school prayer and praying
for the power of God to be released into the human situation while
at the same time embracing the type of politics and public policy
that disabled and disempowered minority groups and the poor.[24]
To be sure, that critique is as relevant today as it was in the 1960s.

The same might be said regarding the meaningfulness and
significance of King's overall philosophy and practice of prayer
and praying. Philosophical, theological, and ethical dialogue with

King around the phenomena of prayer and praying yields insights that can contribute to the overall enrichment of prayer lives today. In the first place, King always stressed the need to be clear about the meaning of prayer, and this could not be more important at a time when the lives of millions lack spiritual focus. People in many parts of this society and the world are experimenting with different religions or seeking new paths to God, and this necessitates some encounter with the question of the meaning of prayer and praying.

King defined prayer variously as an expression of one's faith in God, as the individual's "response to God," as "sincere communication with God," and as "a natural outpouring" of the human spirit. The act of praying for him was an expression of the soul's deepest yearnings or a reaching outward and upward to the supernatural realm for the fulfillment of needs and desires that cannot be met through humanly contrived means.[25] Moreover, King never confined these definitions of prayer and praying to the Christian faith and tradition; he understood that the power released through such exercises of faith extended across religious and doctrinal boundaries.[26] Such a perspective is needed today to counter the spirit of self-righteousness and the religious bigotry and intolerance so often displayed by practitioners of many of the world's great religions.

King also defined prayer and praying as the mainspring of the inner life or as cardinal acts of personal and public piety. In other words, he included prayer and the habit of praying among the essentials of the devotional life, declaring that both, by definition, involve the whole self—mind, soul, spirit, and body. They are the very heart of true worship, especially since they are acts of devout persons that break out into heartfelt praise and thanksgiving.[27] This is indeed instructive for those prone to reduce prayer and the activity of praying to mere ritualism, habit, or tradition. Although King spoke of prayer and the prayerful experience in these terms at times, he knew that the essence of these phenomena demanded a more penetrating understanding and description of what they actually meant in the context of different faith traditions.

King approached the question of the meaning of prayer and praying primarily as a realist and, to some degree, as a philosopher, theologian, and ethicist. When speaking of prayer and the habit of praying as natural tendencies in the human spirit, he was clearly being philosophical. He was the theologian par excellence when talking about prayer and praying as they concerned God or when discussing these devotional activities as appeals to the infinite power and wisdom of God. As an ethicist, King emphasized the effects of prayer and the discipline of praying on human conduct and behavior, the practical side of human life.[28] Here King's thoughts serve as a reminder of the need always to take a well-rounded approach to the meaning of prayer and the activity of praying.

Apparently, the art of prayer and praying for King was largely an exercise of the mind. This should not be surprising given the level of his training and his insistence on employing "the best lights of reason" and keeping "an open and analytical mind" in "the search for truth."[29] Prayer and praying were not, in King's estimation, mindless activities, as atheists typically asserted. At the same time, King was not comfortable with an exclusively intellectual approach to prayer and praying habits, especially the tendency to view prayer as philosophical and theological musings. To be sure, he translated his own understanding of humanity and God into his prayers and practice of praying, but he was always aware of the limitations of his perspective as a human being. There are indeed lessons here for persons of faith who divorce prayer and the experience of praying from the life of the mind and intellect, or who assume that these are strictly spiritual disciplines that require no real effort to think, learn, and analyze.

On another level, King has much to teach us about the importance of taking prayer and the practice of praying seriously while also keeping both in proper perspective. As indicated earlier, King attached great significance to private and public prayer, and he prayed whenever and wherever he felt compelled to do so. His private prayer life, highlighted by the experience of quiet communication with God, nurtured, sustained, and reinforced his spirituality,

King appears at a prayer pilgrimage in Washington, D.C., in 1957.
Courtesy Magnum Photos.

King, Ralph Abernathy, and other civil rights workers kneel in prayer during the campaign in Selma, 1965. Source: UPI/Corbis.

King prays at the grave of Jimmie Lee Jackson in 1965.

Source: Black Star.

King caught "in the grip of an emotion" he could not control while praying during the bus boycott, Montgomery, 1956. Credit: AP/Worldwide Photos. Used with permission.

for it allowed him to continuously listen to God and to be most conscious of the presence of God.[30] Public prayer connected King spiritually and culturally to other believers, to larger communities of faith, and this was equally important in terms of his overall, evolving prayer life. King's reflections on the seriousness of the life of prayer and of praying remain a much-needed challenge to people of faith in the contemporary world.

Any tendency to trivialize prayer and the habit of praying bothered King. He maintained that praying has never been about making trivial requests of God, and he criticized those who used prayer "in an unnatural way." Moreover, King declared that prayer and praying in the most authentic sense are not an escape from inner turmoil or from the worries and anxieties humans face daily. The limitations of the prayer life and of the experience of praying, he held, became more evident when viewed in this manner,[31] or when they were distorted, misappropriated, or misplaced. Such insights are still useful for reviving prayer and the prayerful experience.

Equally significant for humans today is King's charge that the prayerless life is devoid of meaning and therefore not worth living. King taught that the prayerless life is contrary to the very nature of human beings, that it contradicts God's commandments as revealed in Scripture, and that it guarantees estrangement from God. For King, the absence of prayer and praying also inhibited spiritual progress and satisfaction. He held that prayer and the activity of praying must always be one of life's highest priorities, partly because these spiritual resources are mandated by Scripture and modeled in the daily lives and ministries of the ancient prophets, Jesus, and the apostles.[32] In King's thinking, absolutely no human activity could substitute or compensate for the failure to pray. What was most important for him was not a theology or doctrine of prayer but the life of prayer.[33] The untold numbers of people who make the self-comforting and oft-repeated claim that they are too busy to stop and pray daily could benefit immensely from what King shared along these lines.

King's belief that prayers are to be lived as well as uttered affords possibilities for bridging the chasms that too often exist between faith and practice and, more specifically, between doctrinal Christianity and applied or practical Christianity. As King so often suggested, prayer and the experience of praying must be reflected in the way the one who prays lives each day. Prayer and praying for him amounted to merely lifeless and heartless rituals if one resorted to these disciplines every once in a while, when worshiping, or only after some personal tragedy has struck. King's problem with all too many white Christians in the South was that they prayed fervently on Sunday, with hands outstretched to God, while practicing racism and segregation against God's children of color every day of the week.[34] Living prayer daily was, in King's case, a cardinal principle, and this persists as part of his legacy for a nation and a world in which hypocrisy is perhaps more glaringly evident than ever before.

King's idea that intercession is the greatest and truest form of prayer and praying is also meaningful in times when selfishness and self-centeredness have become the standard of human behavior and interaction. Although prayer and praying involve, in some measure, the expression of profound personal longings, King frequently said that prayer and the practice of praying should always begin with an awareness of and emphasis on the presence and needs of others. King categorically discouraged any type of praying restricted to self and to the sphere of personal needs. Self-centered prayer was far less important to him than other-directed prayer. King's own personal prayers and prayer life show that he always lifted others up in prayer,[35] thus providing a model for how we might view and approach the business of prayer and praying in this age.

People worldwide would do well also to revisit King's thoughts on prayer as a path to interfaith dialogue and cooperation. With constant conflict between Christians and Hindus in India, Jews and Muslims in the Middle East, and the Muslim world and the Christian West, King's ideas about interfaith prayer could not be more significant. Some progress in this area is being made in the United States, where Jews, Christians, Muslims, Buddhists, Hindus, and representatives of other faiths have formed panreligious ministerial alliances in which interfaith worship services are held. Representatives of these religious traditions have actually united on national prayer days and on other occasions to pray for peace and unity, and some of these events have been held in memory of King. In India and parts of the Middle East, people of different religious backgrounds are working and praying in unison for mutual understanding and peaceful coexistence between religious rivals, and President Barack Obama has committed himself to easing the tensions between the United States and the Muslim world.[36]

King set a standard that people of various religious persuasions might follow in creating bridges of goodwill, understanding, peaceful coexistence, and cooperation in the interest of the entire human family. King prayed and struggled for freedom, justice, and peace with Protestants, Catholics, Jews, and adherents of other faiths at a time when many still found the idea repulsive. In Selma, Alabama, in 1965, King helped provide the spark that ignited an ecumenical crusade for voting rights on the part of Protestants, Catholics, and Jews. Representatives of these groups formed prayer circles, prayed together, marched together, sang Negro spirituals, and suffered insults and attacks in a spirit of unity and commonality of purpose.[37] King, along with people of many religious affiliations, also cosponsored international campaigns and signed declarations and petitions against apartheid in South Africa and the persecution of the Jews in Russia, all of which recommended prayer as part of the strategy for eliminating social injustice.[38] Ecumenical and interfaith prayer meetings, worship, and cooperation in the United States and other parts of the world today have been inspired to some extent by the movement King led. The ways in which King put prayer and praying to the service of ecumenical and interreligious campaigns for the improvement of the human condition should be studied carefully today for how they might be useful in a post-9/11 world.

In yet another sense, King has much to teach us about the relationship between prayer and the broader struggle for freedom, justice, human dignity, and peace. King believed that the strongest movements for wide-ranging social change had to be conditioned on, sustained, and fashioned by prayer and the art and discipline of praying. Put another way, he saw prayer as a wise and helpful companion on the journey to a better world.[39] At the same time, King saw that prayer had to be somewhat redefined if many were to understand it in the context of a social movement, and so he made prayer a call to action, or a call to movement.[40] Knowing that there were problems in the world that could not be solved by social activism or the advance of human knowledge, particularly as they related to the hearts of people, King developed the habit of joining fellow activists to pray. Thus, he demonstrated how prayer could become a positive force in dealing with the larger social maladies at work in our daily lives.

King really believed that every age should be marked by efforts to apply the far-reaching power and effects of prayer to its own unique set of pressing realities, problems, and challenges. When the most vital elements of prayer are at work in a movement, he asserted, God's mighty hand surcharges and impregnates that movement while bringing it to its richest fruition. This remains part of King's compelling and timeless message. It helps explain the continuing impact of King and the civil rights movement, spiritually and otherwise, on the feminist movement, the peace movement, crusades against abortion and capital punishment, efforts to secure rights for the elderly and handicapped, and the gay rights cause.[41] Moreover, King's message virtually ensures that he will continue to influence debates and discussions about the relationship between spirituality and social transformation.

There is yet another point that could and should be made about King's meaningfulness for contemporary times, especially around the question of the importance and necessity of prayer and praying. King consistently reminded his followers of the tremendous reach of prayer and its vast possibilities and potential, and he convinced many that praying really does work. Genuine prayer and praying are never in vain, King maintained, because God is a trustworthy, dependable being on whom committed human beings can rely.[42] King was convinced that the God of history works through praying human beings, and that the promises of God are fulfilled in response to the prayers of the faithful. This was the basis of much of his hope for the future. It is also a dimension of his challenge to those who struggle today in an uncertain world.

King's prayers and rich legacy of prayer and praying offer still another path to understanding him as a fallible human being who made his life a gift to others. These sources and resources also help us to contemplate prayer and praying in ways that enhance the spiritual journey, for we learn from them the struggles and triumphs of a man who prayed as he lived and lived as he prayed. Due to a vigorous prayer life, King's faith, in the words of L. Harold DeWolf, "was a solid, immovable rock,"[43] an example to which we can look as we struggle with the enduring issues of spiritual life and growth in this new century and millennium.

NOTES

INTRODUCTION

1. Gardner C. Taylor, "King Day Sermon," tape recording, Colgate-Rochester Divinity School, Rochester, New York (January 15, 1974).

2. Clayborne Carson et al., eds., *The Papers of Martin Luther King, Jr.*, vol. 6: *Advocate of the Social Gospel, September 1948–March 1963* (Berkeley: University of California Press, 2007), 410.

3. Psalm 139 was the favorite part of the Bible for the great theologian Howard Thurman, one of King's major intellectual sources and spiritual heroes. The psalmist's references to the God to whom prayer is directed as "the Good Shepherd" struck a responsive chord in King's heart, for it meant that "I shall not want for all of the things which make life worth living." See ibid.; Walter E. Fluker and Catherine Tumber, eds., *A Strange Freedom: The Best of Howard Thurman on Religious Experience and Public Life* (Boston: Beacon, 1998), 158; and Martin Luther King Jr., "'Lost Sheep' or 'The God of the Lost,'" unpublished version of sermon, delivered at Ebenezer Baptist Church, Atlanta, Georgia (September 18, 1966), The Library and Archives of the Martin Luther King Jr. Center for Nonviolent Social Change, Atlanta, Georgia, 2.

4. Carson et al., eds., *Papers of Martin Luther King, Jr.*, 6:93–94, 241–242, 282, and 514; and Clayborne Carson et al., eds., *The Papers of Martin Luther King, Jr.*, vol. 4: *Symbol of the Movement, January 1957–December 1958* (Berkeley: University of California Press, 2000), 108 and 342.

5. Carson et al., eds., *Papers of Martin Luther King, Jr.*, 6:234, 298, 386; and Martin Luther King Jr., "Pharisee and the Publican," unpublished version of sermon, delivered at Ebenezer Baptist Church, Atlanta, Georgia (October 9, 1966), King Center Library and Archives, 4.

6. See Carson, et al., eds., *Papers of Martin Luther King, Jr.*, 6:91, 279–82, 288, 406, 438, 486–87; Martin Luther King Jr., *Strength to Love* (Philadelphia: Fortress Press, 1981 [1963]), 36–37; idem, "The Mission to the Social Frontiers," unpublished version of sermon (n.d.), King Center Library and Archives, 16; idem, "The Ballot: MLK at Zion Hill," unpublished version of interview (July 17, 1962), King Center Library and Archives, 2; idem, "Love and Forgiveness," unpublished version of sermon, delivered to the American Baptist Convention, Atlantic City, New Jersey (May 5, 1964), King Center Library and Archives, 1; and "MLK at Brown Chapel before March," unpublished version of interview, Selma, Alabama (February 1, 1965), King Center Library and Archives, 2.

7. Lewis V. Baldwin, ed., *Never Alone: The Prayers of Martin Luther King, Jr.*, unpublished document (2007), author's files, 25n45.

8. King argued that the Lord's Prayer raised God above the category of "a tribal deity" and established God as a source of life and one to be praised by all humanity. See Carson et al., eds., *Papers of Martin Luther King, Jr.*, 6:486; and Martin Luther King Jr., "Is the Universe Friendly?", unpublished version of sermon, delivered at Ebenezer Baptist Church, Atlanta, Georgia (December 12, 1965), King Center Library and Archives, 5.

9. King also noted that these prayer lines from St. Augustine highlight the conflict between what we actually are and what we know we ought to be. Prayer in this case, then, must always reflect the fact that the Christian life is a process—that we are always in a state of becoming what God would have us be. See Carson et al., eds., *Papers of Martin Luther King, Jr.*, 6:156n26, 190, 335, 424, 554; Clayborne Carson et al., *The Papers of Martin Luther King, Jr.*, vol. 5: *Threshold of a New Decade, January 1959–December 1960* (Berkeley: University of California Press, 2005), 579; King, "Love and Forgiveness," 2, 12; and Martin Luther King Jr., "Lazarus and Dives," unpublished version of sermon, Atlanta, Georgia (March 10, 1963), King Center Library and Archives, 5.

10. This prayer was discovered among King's unpublished papers. In 1963, King was a recipient of the St. Francis Peace Medal, given by the North American Federation of the Third Order of Saint Francis, "in recognition of his truly Christian and Franciscan approach to the civil rights problem through his program of nonviolence." See "A Prayer a Fellow Like Martin Luther King, Junior Would Say," Public Relations Promotions, Ajaye Clarke Associates, San Francisco, California (April 3, 1961), King Center Library and Archives, 1; and "Dr. King's Acceptance Speech," The North American Federation of the Third Order of St. Francis (November 9, 1963), King Center Library and Archives, 1–6. This prayer has also been associated with Mohandas K. Gandhi and Howard Thurman, who were also among King's intellectual and spiritual sources. See Ignatius Jesudasan, S.J., *A Gandhian Theology of Liberation* (Maryknoll, N.Y.: Orbis, 1984), 137; and Howard Thurman, *The Inward Journey: Meditations on the Spiritual Quest* (Richmond, Ind.: Friends United Press, 1977), 104–5.

11. Carson et al., eds., *Papers of Martin Luther King, Jr.*, 6:86, 476.

12. Clayborne Carson et al., eds., *The Papers of Martin Luther King, Jr.*, vol. 1: *Called to Serve, January 1929–June 1951* (Berkeley: University of California Press, 1992), 340.

13. Martin Luther King Jr., "A Knock at Midnight," unpublished version of sermon, delivered at the All Saints Community Church, Los Angeles, California (June 25, 1967), King Center Library and Archives, 1; and Clayborne Carson and Peter Holloran, eds., *A Knock at Midnight: Inspiration from the Great Sermons of Reverend Martin Luther King, Jr.* (New York: Warner, 1998), 65.

14. Carson et al., eds., *Papers of Martin Luther King, Jr.*, 6:97, 223, 410, 590–91.

15. Ibid., 223, 350n1, 293–94; and Baldwin, ed., *Never Alone*, iv.

16. Baldwin, ed., *Never Alone*, ii.

17. Ibid., 1–59.

18. Harold A. Carter, *The Prayer Tradition of Black People* (Valley Forge, Pa.: Judson, 1976), 19.

19. This conclusion is also drawn in Baldwin, ed., *Never Alone*, i–xxvi.

20. Carter, *Prayer Tradition of Black People*, 65–67, 94, 106–13, 129–30.

21. James M. Washington, ed., *Conversations with God: Two Centuries of Prayers by African Americans* (New York: HarperCollins, 1994), 190.

22. O. Richard Bowyer et al., *Prayer in the Black Tradition* (Nashville: Upper Room, 1986), 64–66.

23. The Schomburg Center for Research in Black Culture and The New York Public Library, *Standing in the Need of Prayer: A Celebration of Black Prayer* (New York: Simon and Schuster, 2003), ix–xii, 6, 199, 227, 245, 253.

24. Prayers from King's student days are included, under the title, "A Cry for the Human Condition, 1948–1954," in Baldwin, ed., *Never Alone*, 1–11.

25. Well-chosen quotations from King's student prayers hold the answers to these questions. See ibid.

26. King's sermon prayers are included under the heading, "Toward a Higher Calling and Destiny, 1954–1968," in ibid., 21–38.

27. Unfortunately, the relationship between prayer and preaching, or prayer and sermonizing, in King's life is not given sufficient attention even by scholars who treat him as a homiletician and pulpit artist. See, for examples, Mervyn A. Warren, *King Came Preaching: The Pulpit Power of Dr. Martin Luther King Jr.* (Downers Grove, Ill.: InterVarsity, 2001), 41, 136, 158; Keith D. Miller, *Voice of Deliverance: The Language of Martin Luther King, Jr., and Its Sources* (New York: Free, 1992); Richard Lischer, *The Preacher King: Martin Luther King Jr. and The Word that Moved America* (New York: Oxford University Press, 1995); and Carolyn Calloway-Thomas and John L. Lucaites, eds., *Martin Luther King, Jr., and the Sermonic Power of Public Discourse* (Tuscaloosa: University of Alabama Press, 1993).

28. This is evident from a close study of King's pastoral prayers, which appear under the title "The Controlling Force of Love, 1954–1968," in Baldwin, ed., *Never Alone*, 12–20.

29. Some of King's most powerful movement prayers are brought together under the title "To Be Drum Majors for Justice, 1955–1968," ibid., 39–59.

30. Ibid., 1–59.

1| AN INWARD JOURNEY

1. Clifton H. Johnson, ed., *God Struck Me Dead: Voices of Ex-Slaves* (Cleveland: Pilgrim, 1993 [1969]), 140.

2. Howard Thurman, *The Inward Journey: Meditations on the Spiritual Quest* (Richmond, Ind.: Friends United, 1977 [1961]), 126.

3. Clayborne Carson et al., eds., *The Papers of Martin Luther King, Jr.*, vol. 6: *Advocate of the Social Gospel, September 1948–March 1963* (Berkeley: University of California Press, 2007), 590.

4. The Schomburg Center for Research in Black Culture and The New York Public Library, *Standing in the Need of Prayer: A Celebration of Black Prayer* (New York: Simon and Schuster, 2003), ix (foreword); Johnson, *God Struck Me Dead*, 140.

5. Harold A. Carter, *The Prayer Tradition of Black People* (Valley Forge, Pa.: Judson, 1976), 21, 65–67, 94, 106–13, 129–30; O. Richard Bowyer et al., *Prayer in the Black Tradition* (Nashville: Upper Room, 1986), 9, 64–66; James M. Washington, ed., *Conversations with God: Two Centuries of Prayers by African Americans* (New York: HarperCollins, 1994), 190.

6. Johnson, ed., *God Struck Me Dead*, 15–17, 58, 60, 63; Carter, *Prayer Tradition of Black People*, 23-70; Bowyer et al., *Prayer in the Black Tradition*, 13–15; Washington, ed., *Conversations with God*, 19, 41, 66, 94–95; *Standing in the Need of Prayer*, ix (foreword).

7. Lawrence W. Levine, *Black Culture and Black Consciousness: Afro-American Folk Thought from Slavery to Freedom* (New York: Oxford University Press, 1978), ix (preface).

8. King often said that his introduction to the essentials of the Christian faith first came through his family and home environment, and he most certainly had in mind prayer as a part of this. His paternal grandfather, James King, was not particularly religious, and his maternal grandfather, Adam D. Williams, a Baptist preacher, died when he was only one year old, so neither had a direct influence on his spiritual life. See Martin Luther King Jr., "An Address at the Recognition Dinner for the Nobel Peace Prize," The Dinkler Plaza Hotel, Atlanta, Georgia (January 27, 1965), The Library and Archives of the Martin Luther King, Jr., Center for Nonviolent Social Change, Inc., Atlanta, Georgia, 3; Clayborne Carson

et al., eds., *The Papers of Martin Luther King, Jr.*, vol. 1: *Called to Serve, January 1949–June 1951* (Berkeley: University of California Press, 1992), 360–63; Martin Luther King Jr., *Stride toward Freedom: The Montgomery Story* (New York: Harper & Row, 1958), 21; Lewis V. Baldwin, *There Is a Balm in Gilead: The Cultural Roots of Martin Luther King, Jr.* (Minneapolis: Fortress Press, 1991), 159–64.

    9. See Martin Luther King, Jr., "Thou Fool," unpublished version of sermon, delivered at the Mt. Pisgah Missionary Baptist Church, Chicago, Illinois (August 27, 1967), King Center Library and Archives, 1–2; King, *Stride toward Freedom*, 134; and Carson et al., eds., *Papers of Martin Luther King, Jr.*, 6:590.

    10. Claude F. Jacobs and Andrew J. Kaslow, *The Spiritual Churches of New Orleans* (Knoxville: University of Tennessee Press, 1991), 104.

    11. William F. Allen et al., *Slave Songs in the United States* (New York: Peter Smith, 1951), 35.

    12. Ibid., 97.

    13. Martin Luther King Jr., "Is the Universe Friendly?," unpublished version of sermon, delivered at Ebenezer Baptist Church, Atlanta, Georgia (December 12, 1965), King Center Library and Archives, 5–6, 9; Martin Luther King Jr., "The Meaning of Hope," unpublished version of sermon, delivered at Dexter Avenue Baptist Church, Montgomery, Alabama (December 10, 1967), King Center Library and Archives, 16–17; idem, *Why We Can't Wait* (New York: New American Library, 1964), 61; idem, *Strength to Love* (Philadelphia: Fortress Press, 1981 [1963]), 95; and idem, *Where Do We Go from Here: Chaos or Community?* (Boston: Beacon, 1968), 123.

    14. King argued that the Emancipation Proclamation only left African Americans with "abstract freedom," and he insisted in the 1960s that his people still were not free—that they "still lived a form of slavery disguised by certain niceties of complexity." See King, *Where Do We Go from Here*, 79; and idem, *Why We Can't Wait*, 23.

    15. Mervyn A. Warren, *King Came Preaching: The Pulpit Power of Dr. Martin Luther King Jr.* (Downers Grove, Ill.: InterVarsity, 2001), 136.

    16. "MLK Receiving Tribute from City of Atlanta," unpublished remarks, Atlanta, Georgia (January 28, 1965), King Center Library and

Archives, 1; Carter, *Prayer Tradition of Black People*, 65–67, 94, 106–13, and 129–30.

17. Examples of this type of praying are abundantly evident in Johnson, ed., *God Struck Me Dead*, 13–171.

18. *Standing in the Need of Prayer*, ix (foreword).

19. Ibid.; John H. Blassingame, ed., *Slave Testimony: Two Centuries of Letters, Speeches, Interviews, and Autobiographies* (Baton Rouge: Louisiana State University Press, 1977), 91, 95, 113, 223, 278, 382, 616, 660–61, 673, 689; Thomas L. Webber, *Deep Like the Rivers: Education in the Slave Quarter Community, 1831–1865* (Eugene, Ore.: Wipf & Stock, 2005; originally published in 1978), 162–63, 171; William J. Faulkner, *The Days When the Animals Talked: Black American Folktales and How They Came to Be* (Chicago: Follett, 1977), 30–31; Carter, *Prayer Tradition of Black People*, 19–70.

20. See Martin Luther King Jr., "Ingratitude," unpublished version of a sermon (June 18, 1967), King Center Library and Archives, 8.

21. King, *Stride toward Freedom*, 59–60, 178. This contention is borne out by a careful reading of the more than seventy King prayers in Lewis V. Baldwin, ed., *Never Alone: The Prayers of Martin Luther King Jr.*, unpublished manuscript (2007), author's files, 1–59. Also see Carson et al., eds., *Papers of Martin Luther King, Jr.*, 6:41, 137–39, 421, 429; King, "Thou Fool," 1–4; and Clayborne Carson et al., *The Papers of Martin Luther King, Jr.*, vol. 4: *Symbol of the Movement, January 1957–December 1958* (Berkeley: University of California Press, 2000), 383, 416.

22. King, "Is the Universe Friendly?" 5–9; idem, "Discerning the Signs of History," unpublished version of a sermon, delivered at Ebenezer Baptist Church, Atlanta, Georgia (November 15, 1964), King Center Library and Archives, 4–5; Baldwin, *There Is a Balm in Gilead*, 226–27; idem, *To Make the Wounded Whole: The Cultural Legacy of Martin Luther King, Jr.* (Minneapolis: Fortress Press, 1992), 64–65; King, "Meaning of Hope," 16–17; and King, *Why We Can't Wait*, 61.

23. Albert J. Raboteau, *Slave Religion: The "Invisible Institution" in the Antebellum South* (New York: Oxford University Press, 1978), 213–19; Johnson, ed., *God Struck Me Dead*, 69; and Carter, *Prayer Tradition of Black People*, 26–34.

24. Johnson, ed., *God Struck Me Dead*, 20–21; George P. Rawick, ed., *The American Slave: A Composite Autobiography—Arkansas Narratives*, vol. 10, part 6 (Westport, Conn.: Greenwood, 1972), 64; and Carter, *Prayer Tradition of Black People*, 31–34.

25. Raboteau, *Slave Religion*, 215. For interesting reflections on the significance of the pot as both an African carryover and a part of ceremonial paraphernalia in the invisible institution, see George P. Rawick, ed., *The American Slave: A Composite Autobiography—From Sunup to Sundown* (Westport, Conn.: Greenwood, 1972), 1:42; Carter, *Prayer Tradition of Black People*, 29–30; and Milton C. Sernett, ed., *African American Religious History: A Documentary Witness* (Durham, N.C.: Duke University Press, 1999), 69–74.

26. It would have been virtually impossible for King to be ignorant of such practices, for this author heard his father, the Reverend L. V. Baldwin Sr., speak of a personal "praying ground" that he had as a boy in rural Wilcox County, Alabama. It was typical of the descendants of slaves to delight in having their own "praying ground" as late as the 1930s and 1940s, and King Sr.'s upbringing in rural Stockbridge, Georgia, most certainly exposed him to this practice. For evidence that King knew about the traditions of the invisible institution, see Carson et al., eds., *Papers of Martin Luther King, Jr.*, 1:281.

27. Martin Luther King Jr., "My Dream: Message for My People," unpublished statement prepared for the Associated Negro Press, New York (January 1, 1966), King Center Library and Archives, 1.

28. Harold Courlander, *Negro Folk Music, USA* (New York: Columbia University Press, 1963), 42; and Miles Mark Fisher, *Negro Slave Songs in the United States* (New York: Carol Publishing Group, 1990 [1953]), 66–67.

29. James Weldon Johnson and J. Rosamond Johnson, eds., *The Book of American Negro Spirituals* (New York: Viking, 1926), 89.

30. Carson et al., eds., *Papers of Martin Luther King, Jr.*, 1:281.

31. King credited Du Bois with affording rare insight into how the slaves "learned to sing that most original of all American music, the Negro spiritual," and he undoubtedly came across Du Bois's reflections in his *The Souls of Black Folk*, on the slave preacher, the music, and the frenzy,

those ingredients that, in conjunction with prayer, formed the core of the invisible institution and the slave church. See King, "The Meaning of Hope," 16; and Baldwin, *There Is a Balm in Gilead*, 57. King's familiarity with the scholarship of Du Bois on slave culture is unmistakable, as evidenced in Martin Luther King Jr., "Honoring Dr. DuBois," *Freedomways* 8, no. 2 (Spring 1968): 104–11.

32. Carson et al., eds., *Papers of Martin Luther King, Jr.*, 1:359.

33. Carter, *Prayer Tradition of Black People*, 27–29.

34. King, *Strength to Love*, 62; and Martin Luther King Jr. to the Reverend Jerry M. Chance (May 9, 1961), unpublished letter, King Center Library and Archives, 1.

35. Black prayer has always constituted one form of resistance to injustice and oppression, and King would have understood this. He had a keen sense of the various forms that slave resistance to bondage had assumed, noting that it began with African captives on slave ships and extended to slave cultures in Latin America, the Caribbean, and the United States. See King, "The Meaning of Hope," 13–18.

36. Wilmington newspapers covered activities at the festivals as early as the 1840s, but the most vivid descriptions of their religious side were provided after slavery, as old-timers, many of them ex-slaves, recalled their experiences in earlier times. See *The Delaware State Journal*, Wilmington, Delaware (September 2, 1845), 3; *Blue Hen's Chicken*, Wilmington (September 1, 1848), 2; *The Delaware Gazette*, Wilmington (August 28, 1849), 2; *The Delaware Gazette*, Wilmington (August 27, 1850), 2; and *Every Evening*, Wilmington (August 28, 1882), 1.

37. *Every Evening* (August 28, 1882), 1; *The Delaware State Journal*, Wilmington (August 30, 1883), 1; *The Evening Journal*, Wilmington, Delaware (August 27, 1888), 4; *The Delaware Gazette and State Journal*, Wilmington (August 29, 1889), 3; Lewis V. Baldwin, *"Invisible" Strands in African Methodism: A History of the African Union Methodist Protestant and Union American Methodist Episcopal Churches, 1805–1980* (Metuchen, N.J.: The American Theological Library Association and The Scarecrow Press, 1983), 137–40; idem, *The Mark of a Man: Peter Spencer and the African Union Methodist Tradition* (Lanham, Md.: University

Press of America, 1987), 24–25; idem, "Festivity and Celebration: A Profile of Wilmington's Big Quarterly," *Delaware History* 19, no. 4 (Fall–Winter 1981): 197–211; and *The Morning News*, Wilmington, Delaware (August 30, 1897), 1–3.

38. Baldwin, *"Invisible" Strands in African Methodism*, 213–47; Alice Dunbar-Nelson, *Big Quarterly in Wilmington*, an unpublished essay (1932), the author's files, 1–5; *The Morning News*, Wilmington, Delaware (August 27, 1900), 1; *The Evening Journal*, Wilmington, Delaware (August 26, 1929), 8; and *The Morning News*, Wilmington, Delaware (August 31, 1964), 3.

39. Baldwin, *There Is a Balm in Gilead*, 204; and Pete Seeger and Bob Reiser, *Everybody Says Freedom: A History of the Civil Rights Movement in Songs and Pictures* (New York: W. W. Norton, 1989), 191.

40. *The Morning News*, Wilmington, Delaware (August 26, 1889), 1, 8; Baldwin, *"Invisible" Strands in African Methodism*, 213–39; and idem, *There Is a Balm in Gilead*, 204.

41. See Blassingame, ed., *Slave Testimony*, 673.

42. Carter, *Prayer Tradition of Black People*, 68.

43. This author often heard this spiritual while growing up in the churches of the so-called black belt in rural Alabama, and he was told by his parents and other elders that it had been sung by slaves and their descendants for generations. For other spirituals equally relevant to this line of discussion, see ibid., 65–68.

44. Martin Luther King Jr., "Interruptions," unpublished version of sermon, delivered at Ebenezer Baptist Church, Atlanta, Georgia (January 21, 1968), King Center Library and Archives, 9.

45. King, "Thou Fool," 1–4; and King, *Stride toward Freedom*, 59, 178.

46. As the Alabama ex-slave Henry Baker put it, "Now hit takes a b'liever in God. We so many times ast a m'cle en we don't b'lieve God is gwine tuh do dese things. Now He do whut yuh b'lieve he will do." King undoubtedly heard the same comments about prayer from his grandparents, parents, and other elders while growing up in Atlanta in the 1930s and 1940s. See Blassingame, ed., *Slave Testimony*, 673.

47. Lawrence W. Levine concludes that "it was not merely the spirituals, but the entire network of slave religious practices," including prayer,

"that was undergoing the erosions of change." See Levine, *Black Culture and Black Consciousness*, 164.

48. See Norman R. Yetman, ed., *Life Under the "Peculiar Institution":
Selections from the Slave Narrative Collection* (New York: Holt, Rinehart and Winston, 1970), 264; and Levine, *Black Culture and Black Consciousness*, 137. For similar perspectives, see B. A. Botkin, ed., *Lay My Burden Down: A Folk History of Slavery* (Chicago: University of Chicago Press, 1973 [1945]), 16.

49. Blassingame, ed., *Slave Testimony*, 660.

50. James M. Washington, ed., *A Testament of Hope: The Essential Writings and Speeches of Martin Luther King, Jr.* (New York: HarperCollins, 1991), 217.

51. King once said that "we sing the freedom songs today because the slaves sang them," a point that might also be made concerning the prayers uttered across generations for freedom and deliverance. In other words, King's prayers were also the prayers of his forebears. See King, *Why We Can't Wait*, 61.

52. Blassingame, ed., *Slave Testimony*, 689.

53. The impact of these sources on King's Christian upbringing and spiritual values has been treated at great length in Walter E. Fluker, *They Looked for a City: A Comparative Analysis of the Ideal of Community in the Thought of Howard Thurman and Martin Luther King, Jr.* (Lanham, Md.: University Press of America, 1989), 82–86; Baldwin, *There Is a Balm in Gilead*, 91–206; and Richard Lischer, *The Preacher King: Martin Luther King, Jr. and the Word that Moved America* (New York: Oxford University Press, 1995), 221–42.

54. Carson et al., eds., *Papers of Martin Luther King, Jr.*, 1:359–63; Clayborne Carson, ed., *The Autobiography of Martin Luther King, Jr.* (New York: Warner, 1998), 3–12; Lewis V. Baldwin et al., *The Legacy of Martin Luther King, Jr.: The Boundaries of Law, Politics, and Religion* (Notre Dame, Ind.: University of Notre Dame Press, 2002), 78–79; and Lewis V. Baldwin and Amiri YaSin Al-Hadid, *Between Cross and Crescent: Christian and Muslim Perspectives on Malcolm and Martin* (Gainesville, Fla.: University Press of Florida, 2002), 11–13.

55. Baldwin, *There Is a Balm in Gilead*, 160–74; King, "An Address at the Recognition Dinner," 3; Carson et al., eds., *Papers of Martin Luther*

King, Jr., 1:359–63; and Baldwin and Al-Hadid, *Between Cross and Crescent*, 11–13.

56. Martin Luther King Jr., "Answer to a Perplexing Question," unpublished version of sermon, delivered at Ebenezer Baptist Church, Atlanta, Georgia (March 3, 1963), King Center Library and Archives, 9–10; King, *Strength to Love*, 131–33; and Bowyer et al., *Prayer in the Black Tradition*, 64–66.

57. This was also a part of King's sermonic language or discourse. See Martin Luther King Jr., "A Christian Movement in a Revolutionary Age," unpublished version of a speech (Fall 1966), King Center Library and Archives, 1–2; idem, "A Lecture," unpublished version, delivered under the auspices of The Federation Protestante de France Mutualite, Paris, France (October 24, 1965), King Center Library and Archives, 3–6; and idem, *Strength to Love*, 132. King viewed the Exodus story as the story of all people who struggle for deliverance from bondage, and this had important implications for how he viewed the struggles of both his slave forebears and of African Americans in his own time. He insisted that blacks in his day were still confronting "a form of slavery" because Jim Crow was really slavery "covered up with certain niceties." See Carson et al., eds., *Papers of Martin Luther King, Jr.*, 4:155; and Martin Luther King Jr., "On Interfaith Conference on Civil Rights," unpublished version of statement, Chicago, Illinois (January 15, 1963), King Center Library and Archives, 1.

58. King, *Stride toward Freedom*, 59, 63; idem, *Strength to Love*, 131–33; and Baldwin, ed., *Never Alone*, i–xxiii (general introduction), 1–59.

59. Keith Miller makes a similar claim regarding King's contributions to what he calls "folk preaching"; this insight regarding King and folk praying emerged out of a reading of his groundbreaking work. See Keith D. Miller, *Voice of Deliverance: The Language of Martin Luther King, Jr., and Its Sources* (New York: Free, 1992), 140–41.

60. The employment of prayer as part of the discipline of nonviolence was consistent with King's view of the civil rights movement as "a spiritual movement," or as a movement that drew on "moral and spiritual forces." Prayer was part of that spiritual anvil which grounded the movement. See Washington, ed., *A Testament of Hope*, 84; and Martin

Luther King Jr., "Statement on the Method of Protest in Montgomery, Alabama," unpublished version (March 21, 1956), King Center Library and Archives, 1.

61. Drawing on the nineteenth-century social critic Henry David Thoreau, King stressed the effectiveness of a creative minority who serves the state by resisting it with the goal of transforming it for the better. In King's thinking, the black church was functioning in this capacity in the 1950s and 1960s. See John J. Ansbro, *Martin Luther King, Jr.: The Making of a Mind* (Maryknoll, N.Y.: Orbis, 1982), 111.

62. King viewed "prayer marches" as a spiritual and moral witness against bigotry and intolerance. See Martin Luther King Jr., "Message from Jail," unpublished version, Albany, Georgia (July 14, 1962), King Center Library and Archives, 2.

63. Ibid.; Washington, ed., *A Testament of Hope*, 197; Baldwin, ed., *Never Alone*, 40; King, *Stride toward Freedom*, 87, 137–38, 178; "Why Our Prayer Vigil," Group Statement of the Negotiating Committee of the Albany Movement and Its Chief Consultants, Dr. Martin Luther King, Jr., and Dr. Ralph Abernathy, unpublished version of document, Albany, Georgia (1962), King Center Library and Archives, 1–2; Martin Luther King Jr., "First Ban of Selma March," unpublished version of prayer and statement, Selma, Alabama (March 1965), King Center Library and Archives, 1–2; idem, "Night Vigil," unpublished version of statement, Selma, Alabama (March 13, 1965), King Center Library and Archives, 1; and idem, "The Terrible Cost of the Ballot," unpublished statement (September 1, 1962), King Center Library and Archives, 3.

64. Keith Miller draws the same conclusion with regard to black folk preaching. See Miller, *Voice of Deliverance*, 141.

65. Black preachers like Edward Wilmot Blyden (1832–1912), the West Indian Pan-Africanist, propagandist of emigrationism, and Presbyterian, were known to highlight the importance of interfaith and interreligious concerns in their witness in the United States, but there is no evidence that these preachers stressed and practiced prayer as part of a fabric of interreligious conversation and action in the interest of the common good. See Edward W. Blyden, *Christianity, Islam, and*

the Negro Race (New York: ECA Associates, 1990 [1887]), 1B:232–33, 254–55; and Hollis R. Lynch, *Edward Wilmot Blyden, Pan Negro Patriot, 1832–1912* (New York: Oxford University Press, 1970), 68.

66. Martin Luther King Jr., "An Address to the Synagogue Council of America," unpublished version (December 5, 1965), King Center Library and Archives, 2; idem, "A Lecture," 12; idem, *Where Do We Go from Here?*, 9; and idem, "America's Chief Moral Dilemma," unpublished version of a speech, delivered at the United Church of Christ, General Synod, the Palmer House, Chicago, Illinois (July 6, 1965), King Center Library and Archives, 19.

67. Carson, ed., *The Autobiography of Martin Luther King, Jr.*, 15. As an adult, even King got emotional from time to time while praying. Such was the case during the bus boycott in Montgomery in 1956, when he, in the midst of his prayer, was caught "in the grip of an emotion I could not control." See King, *Stride toward Freedom*, 178.

68. The discussion will be based largely on prayers found in Baldwin, ed., *Never Alone*, 1–11.

2| FROM SHADOWED PLACES

1. James M. Washington, ed., *Conversations with God: Two Centuries of Prayers by African Americans* (New York: HarperCollins, 1994), 15.

2. John Bartlett, *The Shorter Bartlett's Familiar Quotations: A Collection of Passages, Phrases, and Proverbs Traced to their Sources in Ancient and Modern Literature*, ed. Christopher Morley (New York: Pocket, 1964), 92.

3. Clayborne Carson et al., eds., *The Papers of Martin Luther King, Jr.*, vol. 6: *Advocate of the Social Gospel, September 1948–March 1963* (Berkeley: University of California Press, 2007), 590.

4. Clayborne Carson, ed., *The Autobiography of Martin Luther King, Jr.* (New York: Warner, 1998), 13–16; and Martin Luther King Sr. with Clayton Riley, *Daddy King: An Autobiography* (New York: William Morrow, 1980), 75–77, 87, 89.

5. Carson, ed., *The Autobiography of Martin Luther King, Jr.*, 6; Clayborne Carson et al., eds., *The Papers of Martin Luther King, Jr.*, vol. 1:

Called to Serve, January 1929–June 1951 (Berkeley: University of California Press, 1992), 361–63; and King, *Daddy King*, 130.

6. For one who had been nurtured in southern black Baptist fundamentalism almost from birth, King came amazingly close to adopting an uncritical approach to theological liberalism in those early years. See Carson et al., eds., *Papers of Martin Luther King, Jr.*, 1:361–63; King, *Daddy King*, 147; Carson, ed., *The Autobiography of Martin Luther King, Jr.*, 6, 15–16; and Carson et al., eds., *Papers of Martin Luther King, Jr.*, 6:590–91.

7. King embraced the concept of biblical authority but not biblical inerrancy. He saw the virgin birth account as "a mythological story" on the part of the early Christians to highlight Jesus' "moral uniqueness." Hell for him was not a place where the unsaved burned eternally but the state of "being out of fellowship with God." Carson et al., eds., *Papers of Martin Luther King, Jr.*, 6:411; Lee E. Dirks, "The Essence is Love: The Theology of Martin Luther King, Jr.," *The National Observer* (December 30, 1963), 1, 12; and Keith D. Miller, *Voice of Deliverance: The Language of Martin Luther King, Jr., and Its Sources* (New York: Free, 1992), 39–40.

8. Carson, ed., *The Autobiography of Martin Luther King, Jr.*, 16; and King, *Daddy King*, 140–41.

9. Carson, ed., *The Autobiography of Martin Luther King, Jr.*, 16; and Carson et al., eds., *Papers of Martin Luther King, Jr.*, 1:363.

10. King, *Daddy King*, 147. Differences between King Sr. and King Jr. over theological issues proved inevitable, especially since the father was not as well trained and was also a biblical fundamentalist who was suspicious of the evangelical-theological liberalism of his son. See Carson et al., eds., *Papers of Martin Luther King, Jr.*, 1:363.

11. Carson, ed., *The Autobiography of Martin Luther King, Jr.*, 16; Carson et al., eds., *Papers of Martin Luther King, Jr.*, 1:362–63; King, *Daddy King*, 141; and Coretta Scott King, *My Life with Martin Luther King, Jr.* (New York: Henry Holt, 1993 [1969]), 63.

12. It is highly unlikely that King was allowed to do pastoral prayers at such a young age; that privilege at that time was routinely given to senior pastors only. This means that pastoral prayers would have been

left to Daddy King. King Jr. himself would later note that his father made it clear, "Sometimes consciously and sometimes unconsciously," that he was the pastor and his son an assistant minister. See Carson et al., eds., *Papers of Martin Luther King, Jr.*, 1:144; and "Transcript of an Interview with Martin Luther King, Jr.," unpublished version, The Merv Griffin Show, New York (July 6, 1967), The Library and Archives of the Martin Luther King Jr. Center for Nonviolent Social Change, Atlanta, Georgia, 2.

13. King, *My Life with Martin Luther King, Jr.*, 63; and Lewis V. Baldwin, *There Is a Balm in Gilead: The Cultural Roots of Martin Luther King, Jr.* (Minneapolis: Fortress Press, 1991), 280, 286.

14. Carson et al., eds., *Papers of Martin Luther King, Jr.*, 6:570–71; and Lewis V. Baldwin, ed., *Never Alone: The Prayers of Martin Luther King, Jr.*, unpublished manuscript (2007), author's files, 4.

15. Baldwin, ed., *Never Alone*, 2–11; Carson et al., eds., *Papers of Martin Luther King, Jr.*, 1:127, 141, 189–94; and Carson et al., eds., *Papers of Martin Luther King, Jr.*, 6:88, 94, 97, 138–39, 146, 150, 570–71.

16. Ibid., 5–11.

17. Carson et al., eds., *Papers of Martin Luther King, Jr.*, 6:88, 94, 97, 138–39, 146, 150, 570–71; and Clayborne Carson et al., eds., *The Papers of Martin Luther King, Jr.*, vol. 2, *Rediscovering Precious Values, July 1951–November 1955* (Berkeley: University of California Press, 1994), 248, 255–56.

18. Baldwin, ed., *Never Alone*, 2–11. Daddy King was from "the old school" and was known to be, in the language of the black church, "long-winded," even when casually making comments during church services, and this was undoubtedly true of his prayers and sermons as well. King Jr. was slightly irritated at times when his father "would often get up and ramble for ten minutes after he preached, saying nothing." "But," according to Bernard Lee, who would become one of King's close associates in the Southern Christian Leadership Conference (SCLC), "Martin understood. That spirituality just entered into their relationship." Lewis V. Baldwin, private interview with Bernard S. Lee, Washington, D.C. (July 9, 1986); and Baldwin, *There Is a Balm in Gilead*, 317.

19. Carson et al., eds., *Papers of Martin Luther King, Jr.*, 6:94–97; and Baldwin, ed., *Never Alone*, 5.

20. Carson et al., eds., *Papers of Martin Luther King, Jr.*, 6:86–88; and Baldwin, ed., *Never Alone*, 5.

21. Carson et al., eds., *Papers of Martin Luther King, Jr.*, 6:86–88, 94, 97, 137–39, 143, 146, 150, 570–71; Carson et al., eds., *Papers of Martin Luther King, Jr.*, 2:248, 255–56; Carson et al., eds., *Papers of Martin Luther King, Jr.*, 1:127, 141, 189–94, 290; and Baldwin, ed., *Never Alone*, 2–11.

22. Carson et al., eds., *Papers of Martin Luther King, Jr.*, 6:143–46; and Baldwin, ed., *Never Alone*, 6.

23. Aside from King's early sermons, these six prayers are perhaps the best source for understanding the dimensions of his spiritual life as a student. They can be found in Carson et al., eds., *Papers of Martin Luther King, Jr.*, 6:137–39. For an analytical treatment of the prayers, the reader is referred to Baldwin, ed., *Never Alone*, 7–10.

24. King, *My Life with Martin Luther King, Jr.*, 63; Carson et al., eds., *Papers of Martin Luther King, Jr.*, 6:137–39, 570; and Carson et al., eds., *Papers of Martin Luther King, Jr.*, 2:314.

25. Unfortunately, the impact of King's experiences at Calvary and Twelfth Baptist, black congregations in the Northeast, on the development of his spiritual life as a whole has been completely ignored, even by King scholars who treat King's oratorical gifts and style as a preacher. See Baldwin, *There Is a Balm in Gilead*, 125, 277, 282–85, 302; and Carson et al., *Papers of Martin Luther King, Jr.*, 1:47, 53, 125n, 161, 330, 332.

26. While at Crozer, King actually made this assessment of religion in general, but it is most certainly reflective of his views on prayer. At other points in his writings at Crozer, he referred to religion as a part of the entire continuum of life's issues, which would of course include prayer. See Carson et al., eds., *Papers of Martin Luther King, Jr.*, 6:72; and Carson et al., eds., *Papers of Martin Luther King, Jr.*, 1:363, 384. Also see Martin Luther King Jr., *Stride toward Freedom: The Montgomery Story* (New York: Harper & Row, 1958), 35–36.

27. King would also describe his call to preach in these terms, thus offering some suggestion of how prayer and preaching came together in his consciousness in those early years. See Carson et al., eds., *Papers*

of Martin Luther King, Jr., 6:154; Martin Luther King Jr., "My Call to Preach," unpublished version of document, stated before the American Baptist Convention (August 7, 1959); The Martin Luther King Jr. Papers, Special Collections, Mugar Memorial Library, Boston University, Boston, Massachusetts, 1; and Baldwin, *There Is a Balm in Gilead*, 279–80.

28. King categorically rejected Karl Barth's conception of God as "Wholly Other" as well as Aristotle's view of God as oblivious to human affairs. See Carson et al., eds., *Papers of Martin Luther King, Jr.*, 1:232, 281, 294, 413; and John J. Ansbro, *Martin Luther King, Jr.: The Making of a Mind* (Maryknoll, N.Y.: Orbis, 1982), 46–47. Quoting Brightman, King the seminarian asserted that the experience of prayer constitutes that moment in which "the religious person comes into actual and immediate relation with the divine being." See Edgar S. Brightman, *A Philosophy of Religion* (New York: Prentice-Hall, 1940), 82.

29. Carson et al., eds., *Papers of Martin Luther King, Jr.*, 1:290.

30. One could argue that this was the case even before King arrived at Boston, for he was introduced to a kind of "homespun personalism" in the King home and at Ebenezer Baptist Church long before he became a college student. See Carson et al., eds., *Papers of Martin Luther King, Jr.*, 6:137–39, 146, 150, 154; and Baldwin, ed., *Never Alone*, 6–11. The term "homespun personalism" comes from, and is thoroughly developed by, Rufus Burrow Jr., *God and Human Dignity: The Personalism, Theology, and Ethics of Martin Luther King, Jr.* (Notre Dame, Ind.: University of Notre Dame Press, 2006), 70.

31. Carson et al., eds., *Papers of Martin Luther King, Jr.*, 1:127, 141.

32. Ibid., 189–94.

33. King quoted Jeremiah as much and probably more than he did any other Hebrew prophet, in part because so much of what he said about hope registered well with the black experience. See ibid., 191–92; Martin Luther King Jr., "The Meaning of Hope," unpublished version of sermon, Dexter Avenue Baptist Church, Montgomery, Alabama (December 10, 1967), King Center Library and Archives, 16–17; and Lewis V. Baldwin, *To Make the Wounded Whole: The Cultural Legacy of Martin Luther King, Jr.* (Minneapolis: Fortress Press, 1992), 64–65.

34. Carson et al., eds., *The Papers of Martin Luther King, Jr.*, 1:255, 259.

35. Ibid., 387.

36. Here King alluded to the connection between prayer and mystical experience, an issue he had raised at greater length in his paper on "The Significant Contributions of Jeremiah to Religious Thought" at Crozer. See Carson et al., eds., *Papers of Martin Luther King, Jr.*, 2:81; and William E. Hocking, *The Meaning of God in Human Experience* (New Haven: Yale University Press, 1912), 439.

37. Carson et al., eds., *Papers of Martin Luther King, Jr.*, 2:76–92.

38. Interestingly enough, Philip Lenud, one of King's classmates in college, recalled that King "didn't dwell too much on metaphysics"; he was more "concerned with the pragmatics of existence." This point is relevant to any serious discussion of King's approach to prayer and the prayer life. See Lewis V. Baldwin, private interview with Philip Lenud, Nashville, Tennessee (April 7, 1987); and Baldwin, *There Is a Balm in Gilead*, 300–301.

39. Quoting Thomas Carlyle, King variously described prayer as "indigenous to the human spirit" and central to "the native and deepest impulse of the soul of man." He also pulled back on Samuel Johnson's assertion that "there is no argument for prayer," especially since it is "the natural response" of humans to the God of history and the universe. At the same time, King, unlike the evangelical and fundamentalist Christians, appreciated the questions raised by atheists, because they were, in his estimation, a challenge to the tendency toward a complacent theism. See Carson et al., eds., *Papers of Martin Luther King, Jr.*, 6:590; and Harry Emerson Fosdick, *The Meaning of Prayer* (New York: Association Press, 1949), 1.

40. Carson et al., eds., *Papers of Martin Luther King, Jr.*, 6:590.

41. Ibid. Also see Martin Luther King Jr., "Answer to a Perplexing Question," unpublished version of sermon, Atlanta, Georgia (March 3, 1963), King Center Library and Archives, 9–11; O. Richard Bowyer et al., *Prayer in the Black Tradition* (Nashville: Upper Room, 1986), 64–65; and Baldwin, ed., *Never Alone*, xx.

42. Martin Luther King Jr., *Strength to Love* (Philadelphia: Fortress Press, 1981 [1963]), 131–32.

43. Carson et al., eds., *The Papers of Martin Luther King, Jr.*, 6:590–91.

44. Significantly, King was writing this and other papers on prayer at essentially the same time he was involved in an intense "intellectual quest

for a method to eliminate social evil." That "quest" had actually begun at Morehouse, and it became more "serious" at Crozer and Boston. See Carson, ed., *The Autobiography of Martin Luther King, Jr.*, 17.

45. King used the term, "cooperate with God's prayer," which is understood in this work as a challenge to and call for pray-ers to become coworkers with God in making prayer an enriching and fruitful exercise. This divine-human partnership in making prayer answerable and effective in life situations is also suggested in King's contention that prayer should always be "a supplement" to our persistent, feeble efforts and not "a substitute" for them. See Carson et al., eds., *Papers of Martin Luther King, Jr.*, 6:590.

46. From all indications, King held this view throughout his life. Harold Carter writes: "I once heard Dr. King say in a sermon on nonviolence that the one who prays ought to work as though the answer to one's prayers depended upon oneself and not totally upon the power of God." See Harold A. Carter, "The Living Legacy of Dr. Martin Luther King, Jr. as Seen through the Streams of Prayer: Psalms 1:3," in *No Other Help I Know: Sermons on Prayer and Spirituality*, ed. J. Alfred Smith Sr. (Valley Forge, Pa.: Judson, 1996), 11.

47. King's effort to unite head and heart, the cognitive and the affective, in his prayers as in his sermons was actually his way of bringing together the resources of his heritage and the fruits of his academic training. See Baldwin, *There Is a Balm in Gilead*, 296n77. Coretta Scott King put it another way, insisting that "the balance between mind and soul, intellect and emotion," was what King struggled "to achieve." See King, *My Life with Martin Luther King, Jr.*, 83.

48. It was virtually impossible for King to avoid the thought that he was born for something really special because his parents and many of his friends expected greatness from him, and he frequently heard this while pursuing his studies at Morehouse, Crozer, and Boston. See Carson et al., eds., *Papers of Martin Luther King, Jr.*, 1:121, 334, 354 ; Carson et al., eds., *Papers of Martin Luther King, Jr.*, 2:163; and Lewis V. Baldwin and Amiri YaSin Al-Hadid, *Between Cross and Crescent: Christian and Muslim Perspectives on Malcolm and Martin* (Gainesville: University Press of Florida, 2002), 28.

49. Some twenty-seven of King's sermonic prayers can be found in Baldwin, ed., *Never Alone*, 21–38.

3| TREMBLES IN THE BREAST

1. John Bartlett, *The Shorter Bartlett's Familiar Quotations: A Collection of Passages, Phrases, and Proverbs Traced to Their Sources in Ancient and Modern Literature*, ed. Christopher Morley (New York: Pocket, 1964), 259.

2. James M. Washington, ed., *Conversations with God: Two Centuries of Prayers by African Americans* (New York: HarperCollins, 1994), 6.

3. Martin Luther King Jr., *Strength to Love* (Philadelphia: Fortress Press, 1981 [1963]), 155.

4. The absence of attention to prayer as a major ingredient in King's sermon craft and art of preaching, especially by major King scholars, is inexcusable; this is what explains the essence of King and how he understood his mission in the church, society, and the world. Fleeting attention to the subject is given in Mervyn A. Warren, *King Came Preaching: The Pulpit Power of Dr. Martin Luther King Jr.* (Downers Grove, Ill.: InterVarsity, 2001), 136, 158.

5. Warren makes this point emphatically, noting that "King's prayer habit was a continual source of spiritual power and confidence and, in consequence, general sermon preparation." Warren also suggests that a part of King's special "Day of Silence and Meditation," or "Prayer and Meditation," set aside each week, was devoted to preparing sermons. See ibid. Wyatt Walker, former chief of staff to King, also refers to this "Day of Silence" as part of King's routine, but makes no mention of sermon preparation. Walker reports that the day was devoted to silent prayer and meditation and also to planning strategy for the nonviolent campaigns King had to lead in the segregated South. There is some truth in the claims of both Warren and Walker. This was noted in a letter from Wyatt Tee Walker to Lewis V. Baldwin (April 30, 2009).

6. Martin Luther King Jr., *Stride toward Freedom: The Montgomery Story* (New York: Harper & Row, 1958), 59–63.

7. Ibid.; and Harold A. Carter, *The Prayer Tradition of Black People* (Valley Forge, Pa.: Judson, 1976), 106–7.

8. Ibid.; and King, *Stride toward Freedom*, 59–63. This point by King requires some clarification. King did not mean that the preacher should disregard the need to study and prepare while simply praying and

depending on God. On one occasion he reminded black preachers that it was senseless to spend a lot of time trying "to learn how to whoop and holler." "We've got to study some," he added. King knew that preaching at its best required both divine grace and human initiative, which meant that the preacher had to pray while also studying intensely to ensure that his sermons had substance in terms of content and biblical and theological backbone. Also, King believed that the preacher had to study hard in order to understand the difference between "Good History" (what God has already done in the past) and "Good News" (what God is doing today). Otherwise, it was virtually impossible for a sermon to be truly relevant and effective. For King, then, making the gospel and the biblical revelation relevant required more than "staying on bended knees" or bowing before the God who "makes a way out of no way." See King, *Strength to Love*, 131–33; Clayborne Carson et al., eds., *The Papers of Martin Luther King, Jr.*, vol. 6: *Advocate of the Social Gospel, September 1948–March 1963* (Berkeley: University of California Press, 2007), 223–24; Martin Luther King Jr., "Transformed Non-Conformist," unpublished version of sermon, Ebenezer Baptist Church, Atlanta, Georgia (January 16, 1966), The Library and Archives of the Martin Luther King Jr. Center for Nonviolent Social Change, Atlanta, Georgia, 9; Clayborne Carson et al., eds., *The Papers of Martin Luther King, Jr.*, vol. 4: *Symbol of the Movement, January 1957–December 1958* (Berkeley: University of California Press, 2000), 338; and Clayborne Carson and Peter Holloran, eds., *A Knock at Midnight: Inspiration from the Great Sermons of Reverend Martin Luther King, Jr.* (New York: Warner, 1998), 106.

9. King, *Stride toward Freedom*, 59, 134–35. Harold Carter highlights the importance of the home and other private spaces as a context for secret prayers in the development of the black prayer tradition in all of its variety, complexity, and wholeness. See Carter, *The Prayer Tradition of Black People*, 30–34, 75–76.

10. Asking visiting preachers to preach on the spur of the moment has long been a habit of pastors in the black church, but King was always apt to decline the request because he believed in careful study and prayerful preparation as a precondition for preaching. He knew that there were always black preachers, especially the "jack leg" type or

those desperately seeking to become pastors, who literally jumped at the opportunity to preach at any moment, depending solely on the power of their voice and antics to be effective, or to bring listeners to the high pitch of emotional participation. King vehemently criticized this tendency, especially the type of preacher who depended on "the volume of his voice rather than the content of his message" and who paraded as a "mere showman," giving "people what they want rather than what they need." In such situations, he noted sadly, the church becomes a mere "entertainment center." At the same time, King respected the raw, natural talent of the untutored or untrained black preacher, his spiritual resources and significance as a cultural figure, or as one who figured prominently in the orally transmitted expressive culture of the Negro community. Like Benjamin E. Mays, his mentor at Morehouse College, King imbibed much of his measured speaking rhythm from listening to the nonlettered Negro preachers in the South, many of whom mastered the modes of eloquence. King's ability to "whoop" or "tune up" at times owed much to this tradition, which had roots in slavery. See Lawrence E. Carter Sr., ed., *Walking Integrity: Benjamin Elijah Mays, Mentor to Martin Luther King, Jr.* (Macon, Ga.: Mercer University Press, 1998), 14; Coretta Scott King, *My Life with Martin Luther King, Jr.* (New York: Henry Holt, 1993 [1969]), 83, 95; and Lewis V. Baldwin, *There Is a Balm in Gilead: The Cultural Roots of Martin Luther King, Jr.* (Minneapolis: Fortress Press, 1991), 285–86.

11. Warren, *King Came Preaching*, 158.

12. Sensing his utter dependence on God, King was always prayerful when preaching, regardless of the arena in which he found himself. He developed a rhythm of prayer in his life which, like that of his sermons, deepened his experiences and relationship with what he called his "cosmic companion." See King, *Stride toward Freedom*, 59; Carson et al., eds., *Papers of Martin Luther King, Jr.*, 4:249; and Lewis V. Baldwin, ed., *Never Alone: The Prayers of Martin Luther King Jr.*, unpublished manuscript (2007), author's files, 30.

13. In the tradition of the black church, this actually constitutes a part of what Clifton Johnson calls "the warming up period" that precedes the actual sermon, though Johnson fails to make the point with emphasis

or clarity. Rousing prayers before the sermon, especially in King's time, were believed to hasten what Johnson terms "the coming of the spirit," without which sound preaching was considered impossible. See Clifton Johnson, ed., *God Struck Me Dead: Voices of Ex-Slaves* (Cleveland: Pilgrim, 1993 [1969]), 5–6.

14. Clayborne Carson et al., eds., *The Papers of Martin Luther King, Jr.*, vol. 2: *Rediscovering Precious Values, July 1951–November 1955* (Berkeley: University of California Press, 1994), 287; Baldwin, *There Is a Balm in Gilead*, 275–87; and Lewis V. Baldwin, "The Minister as Preacher, Pastor, and Prophet: The Thinking of Martin Luther King, Jr.," *American Baptist Quarterly* 7, no. 2 (June 1988): 94n4.

15. This is a common phrase in prayers offered in the black church; it is in reference to the man who is scheduled to preach on a particular Sunday morning. Routinely, God's blessings are solicited on behalf of "the man who is to stand in the shoes of John." See Baldwin, *There Is a Balm in Gilead*, 273.

16. King, *Stride toward Freedom*, 63.

17. Martin Luther King Jr., *Why We Can't Wait* (New York: New American Library, 1964), 67.

18. William Jones identifies "the posture of freedom and fearlessness" as one of the major characteristics of the black preaching tradition. The same might be said of the black prayer tradition, which King exemplified so supremely. See William R. Jones, "The Art of Preaching from a Black Perspective," unpublished paper (n.d.), the author's files, 7–9; and Baldwin, *There Is a Balm in Gilead*, 291–98.

19. Clayborne Carson et al., eds., *The Papers of Martin Luther King, Jr.*, vol. 1: *Called to Serve, January, 1929–June 1951* (Berkeley: University of California Press, 1992), 181, 190–92; Martin Luther King Jr., "Pharisee and Publican," unpublished version of sermon, Atlanta, Georgia (October 9, 1966), King Center Library and Archives, 1–5; idem, "An Address," The Synagogue Council of America (December 5, 1965), King Center Library and Archives, 9–10; Carson et al., eds., *Papers of Martin Luther King, Jr.*, 6:93–94, 180, 203–5, 241, 486–92; Rabbi Marc Schneier, *Shared Dreams: Martin Luther King, Jr., and the Jewish Community* (Woodstock, Vt.: Jewish Lights, 1999), 32; James M. Washington, ed.,

A *Testament of Hope: The Essential Writings and Speeches of Martin Luther King, Jr.* (New York: HarperCollins, 1991), 481; and Baldwin, *There Is a Balm in Gilead*, 327–29.

20. King undoubtedly had this in mind when he asserted that "the preacher must be concerned about the whole man," or the spiritual, material, intellectual, and psychological needs of the entire person. This sense of the preacher and the preached word was passed down from his father and maternal grandfather, Martin King Sr. and A. D. Williams. See Carson and Holloran, eds., *A Knock at Midnight*, 146; King, *Stride toward Freedom*, 35–36; and Martin Luther King Sr. with Clayton Riley, *Daddy King: An Autobiography* (New York: William Morrow, 1980), 82.

21. To illustrate the futility of ineffective preaching, King joked at times about the church member who becomes preoccupied with the power of the preacher's voice and performance in the pulpit while essentially ignoring the content of the message. Such a member is apt to say, "He sure did preach this morning," but when asked about what the preacher actually said, he or she responds: "I don't know but he sure did preach this morning." King was always attempting to make a serious point here; namely, that a prayerful and substantive sermon has staying and transforming power. See Carson et al., eds., *Papers of Martin Luther King, Jr.*, 6:223–24.

22. King, *Stride toward Freedom*, 206–9; Carson and Holloran, eds., *A Knock at Midnight*, 146; and Carson et al., eds., *Papers of Martin Luther King, Jr.*, 6:224.

23. One might argue that this is rather typical in the black church tradition. Prayer is never merely one element of sermonizing. For the preacher who preaches, it is in some measure a form of sermonizing itself. For examples of how King's sermons were sprinkled with prayers, see Carson et al., eds., *Papers of Martin Luther King, Jr.*, 6:88, 91, 93–94, 224, 405.

24. Clifton Johnson offers rich insights into how the black preacher has traditionally encouraged prayerful preaching as a participative exercise. During the warming-up phase of the sermon, he writes, "the preacher speaks from the scriptures and on the whole presents a sound argument, making

practical applications to everyday life." "All this time," Johnson continues, "he is calling upon the members, saying 'Pray with me a little while children,' etc. He is feeling his way until the spirit strikes him." Obviously, King was an heir of this tradition, and his brand of dialogical and prayerful preaching reflected that tradition in powerful and unique ways. See Johnson, ed., *God Struck Me Dead*, 5; and Baldwin, *There Is a Balm in Gilead*, 292–94.

25. Abundant evidence of how King exploited the dialogical character of both prayer and preaching in the sacred space of the pulpit is offered in Carson and Holloran, eds., *A Knock at Midnight*, 6–19, 86–100, 106–15, 121–39, 147–64; Carson et al., eds., *Papers of Martin Luther King, Jr.*, 6:438–42, 444–54, 533–34; Clayborne Carson et al., eds., *The Papers of Martin Luther King, Jr.*, vol. 3: *Birth of a New Age, December 1955–December 1956* (Berkeley: University of California Press, 1997), 71–79; Clayborne Carson et al., eds., *The Papers of Martin Luther King, Jr.*, vol. 5: *Threshold of a New Decade, January 1959–December 1960* (Berkeley: University of California Press, 2005), 359–63.

26. William R. Jones, the African American philosopher of religion, has written brilliantly about "the dialogical character" of preaching in the black tradition, and his reflections are quite useful for situating King in this tradition. See Jones, "The Art of Preaching from a Black Perspective," 7–9; and Baldwin, *There Is a Balm in Gilead*, 291–95.

27. Johnson, ed., *God Struck Me Dead*, 5; and Carson et al., eds., *Papers of Martin Luther King, Jr.*, 4:316.

28. King, *Stride toward Freedom*, 134–35; Carson and Holloran, eds., *A Knock at Midnight*, 160–63; and Baldwin, *There Is a Balm in Gilead*, 292–93.

29. Carson and Holloran, eds., *A Knock at Midnight*, 159–60; and Baldwin, *There Is a Balm in Gilead*, 293.

30. Martin Luther King Jr., "An Address," The Freedom Fund Report Dinner, Fifty-third Annual Convention of the NAACP, Atlanta, Georgia (July 5, 1962), King Center Library and Archives, 1; idem, "An Address," Mass Meeting, Grenada, Mississippi (March 19, 1968), King Center Library and Archives, 1; and idem, "An Address," Mass Meeting, Augusta, Georgia (March 22, 1968), King Center Library and Archives, 3.

31. Martin Luther King Jr., "A Knock at Midnight," unpublished version of sermon, Canaan Baptist Church, New York, New York (March 24, 1968), King Center Library and Archives, 1; and Baldwin, *There Is a Balm in Gilead*, 294. One of the best treatments of the Negro preacher and the various devices to which he resorted to get responses from church folk is John Dollard, *Caste and Class in a Southern Town* (New York: Doubleday, 1957), 240–41.

32. King, "An Address," Mass Meeting, Augusta, Georgia, 1; idem, "Rally Speech," Georgia Tour of Pre-Washington Campaign, Albany, Georgia (March 22, 1968), King Center Library and Archives, 1; idem, "An Address," Mass Meeting, Macon, Georgia (March 22, 1968), King Center Library and Archives, 1; and Baldwin, *There Is a Balm in Gilead*, 293–94.

33. King's cultural significance and influence, particularly in mastering the oral traditions of the black folk church, is treated in Baldwin, *There Is a Balm in Gilead*, 275–95; and Keith D. Miller, "Martin Luther King, Jr., and the Black Folk Pulpit," *The Journal of American History* 78, no. 1 (June 1991): 120–23.

34. See, for an example, Carolyn Calloway-Thomas and John L. Lucaites, eds., *Martin Luther King, Jr., and the Sermon Power of His Public Discourse* (Tuscaloosa: The University of Alabama Press, 1993).

35. Jonathan Rieder, *The Word of the Lord Is Upon Me: The Righteous Performance of Martin Luther King, Jr.* (Cambridge, Mass.: Belknap Press of Harvard University Press, 2008).

36. Keith D. Miller, *Voice of Deliverance: The Language of Martin Luther King, Jr., and Its Sources* (New York: Free Press, 1992).

37. Richard Lischer, *The Preacher King: Martin Luther King Jr. and the Word That Moved America* (New York: Oxford University Press, 1995).

38. Martin Luther King Jr., "The UnChristian Christian: SCLC Looks Closely at Christianity in a Troubled Land," *Ebony* 20, no. 10 (August 1965): 77; Lischer, *The Preacher King*, 3; and Baldwin, *There Is a Balm in Gilead*, 273.

39. This becomes abundantly clear from even a cursory reading of King's sermonic prayers in Baldwin, ed., *Never Alone*, 2–11.

40. Carson et al., eds., *The Papers of Martin Luther King, Jr.*, 6:265, 307; and Baldwin, ed., *Never Alone*, 25n24.

41. Carson et al., eds., *Papers of Martin Luther King, Jr.*, 6:270, 303, 307, 391; Carson et al., eds., *Papers of Martin Luther King, Jr.*, 5:156–57; and Baldwin, ed., *Never Alone*, 24, 29, 33.

42. Carson et al., eds., *Papers of Martin Luther King, Jr.*, 6:265, 307; and Baldwin, ed., *Never Alone*, 25n24. For brilliant insights on King's understanding of the creative and productive life, see Michael G. Long, *Martin Luther King Jr. on Creative Living* (St. Louis: Chalice, 2004), 1–135. For King's own extensive reflections on the subject, see his sermon, "The Dimensions of a Complete Life," in Martin Luther King Jr., *The Measure of a Man* (Philadelphia: Fortress Press, 1988 [1959]), 33–56. Interestingly enough, King ends the sermon, "The Dimensions of a Complete Life," with a prayer that speaks as forcefully as the sermon to the need for a well-rounded life.

43. Carson et al., eds., *Papers of Martin Luther King, Jr.*, 6:280, 283, 437; and Baldwin, ed., *Never Alone*, 27n28. Echoes of these same thoughts course through Long, *Martin Luther King Jr. on Creative Living*, 1–135.

44. Carson et al., eds., *Papers of Martin Luther King, Jr.*, 6:280, 283; Martin Luther King Jr., "A Challenge to the Churches and Synagogues," in *Race: Challenge to Religion*, ed. Mathew Ahmann (Chicago: Henry Regnery, 1963), 168–69; Martin Luther King Jr., "Speech at an SCLC Staff Retreat," unpublished version (May 2–3, 1967), King Center Library and Archives, 31–32; Carson et al., eds., *Papers of Martin Luther King, Jr.*, 5:156; and David J. Garrow, *Bearing the Cross: Martin Luther King Jr. and the Southern Christian Leadership Conference* (New York: William Morrow, 1986), 135, 142–44, 171.

45. King, *Strength to Love*, 36–46; Carson and Holloran, eds., *A Knock at Midnight*, 37–60; and King, *Stride toward Freedom*, 88, 102–7.

46. Carson et al., eds., *Papers of Martin Luther King, Jr.*, 6:338, 346, 421, 429; Baldwin, ed., *Never Alone*, 32–33, 35–38; King, *The Measure of a Man*, 31, 56; and Carson et al., eds., *Papers of Martin Luther King, Jr.*, 5:571, 579.

47. Carson et al., eds., *Papers of Martin Luther King, Jr.*, 6:591.

48. Carson et al., eds., *Papers of Martin Luther King, Jr.*, 4:166–67; Carson et al., eds. *Papers of Martin Luther King, Jr.*, 5:145, 156–57; Carson and Holloran, eds., *A Knock at Midnight*, 186; and Clayborne Carson and Kris Shepard, eds., *A Call to Conscience: The Landmark Speeches of Dr. Martin Luther King, Jr.* (New York: Warner, 2001), 40–41. King was deeply committed to the shaping of what he called "a new kind of man" through a revolution of values and priorities, and he was not likely to exclude prayer from this kind of crusade or mission. See "Doubts and Certainties Link," unpublished transcript of an interview with Martin Luther King Jr., London, England (Winter 1968), King Center Library and Archives, 5; Martin Luther King Jr., *Where Do We Go from Here: Chaos or Community?* (Boston: Beacon, 1968), 186–91; and Lewis V. Baldwin, *To Make the Wounded Whole: The Cultural Legacy of Martin Luther King, Jr.* (Minneapolis: Fortress Press, 1992), 286.

49. Baldwin, ed., *Never Alone*, xi; and Warren, *King Came Preaching*, 136–37, 158.

50. This is evident from even a cursory reading of King's sermonic prayers. See Baldwin, ed., *Never Alone*, 24–38.

51. Robert M. Franklin Jr., "Martin Luther King Jr. as Pastor," *The Iliff Review* 42, no. 2 (Spring 1985), 4–20.

4| BEFORE WHOM ANGELS BOW

1. James M. Washington, ed., *Conversations with God: Two Centuries of Prayers by African Americans* (New York: HarperCollins, 1994), 30.

2. George A. Buttrick, *Prayer* (New York: Abingdon, 1941), 35–36.

3. Martin Luther King Jr., *Strength to Love* (Philadelphia: Fortress Press, 1981 [1963]), 112.

4. Patrick Coy insists that King "was an American pastor who cared deeply about the soul of his nation." To be sure, King's activities as pastor of a congregation and as a national and world leader were interrelated, thus necessitating a dialectical approach to his pastoral role. See Earl E. Shelp and Ronald H. Sunderland, eds., *The Pastor as Prophet* (New York: Pilgrim, 1985), 15.

5. Referring to a particular praying moment during his years at Dexter, King declared that he "discovered then" that "religion had to become real" to him, and he "had to know God" for himself. See Clayborne Carson and Peter Holloran, eds., *A Knock at Midnight: Inspiration from the Great Sermons of Reverend Martin Luther King, Jr.* (New York: Warner, 1998), 162; and Lewis V. Baldwin, *There Is a Balm in Gilead: The Cultural Roots of Martin Luther King, Jr.* (Minneapolis: Fortress Press, 1991), 188. King's leadership and experiences as senior pastor at Dexter Avenue Baptist Church have not been treated seriously in the scholarship. Any serious treatment of the subject requires some attention to Wally G. Vaughn and Richard W. Wills, eds., *Reflections on Our Pastor: Dr. Martin Luther King, Jr., at Dexter Avenue Baptist Church, 1954–1960* (Dover, Mass.: Majority Press, 1999), 18–21, 24, 27, 92; and Michael Thurman, ed., *Voices from the Dexter Pulpit* (Montgomery, Ala.: NewSouth, 2001), 27–35.

6. Carson and Holloran, eds., *A Knock at Midnight*, 161; and Martin Luther King Jr., *Stride toward Freedom: The Montgomery Story* (New York: Harper & Row, 1958), 59, 133–35, 138–39, and 177–78.

7. This insight owes much to Gaylord Noyce's claim that prayer is one form that pastoral conversation takes and that it is a basic but unique vehicle in the pastor's relationship with God. Noyce further notes that pastoral conversation can also assume the form of preaching, moral discourse, and counseling. Noyce's emphasis on prayer as an essential aspect of the art of pastoral conversation is taken seriously in this examination of King's prayer life as a pastor. See Gaylord Noyce, *The Art of Pastoral Conversation* (Atlanta: John Knox, 1981), 111–16; King, *Stride toward Freedom*, 59, 134–35, 178; and Vaughn and Wills, eds., *Reflections on Our Pastor*, 19, 55, 65.

8. Vaughn and Wills, eds., *Reflections on Our Pastor*, 19, 55, 65; and King, *Stride toward Freedom*, 59, 137–38, 178.

9. Vaughn and Wills, eds., *Reflections on Our Pastor*, 19, 55, 65; and Lewis V. Baldwin, ed., *Never Alone: The Prayers of Martin Luther King, Jr.* unpublished manuscript (2007), author's files, 12–20.

10. At Dexter, King was known not only as a praying pastor but a "fighting pastor" as well. All of this figured into what he termed his "great

and creative spiritual venture" at the Dexter Avenue Baptist Church. See Vaughn and Wills, eds., *Reflections on Our Pastor*, 19, 55, 65; King, *Stride toward Freedom*, 177–78; Baldwin, ed., *Never Alone*, 13–20; Clayborne Carson et al., eds., *The Papers of Martin Luther King, Jr.*, vol. 4: *Symbol of the Movement, January 1957–December 1958* (Berkeley: University of California Press, 2000), 227, 241, 311; and Clayborne Carson et al., eds., *The Papers of Martin Luther King, Jr.*, vol. 5: *Threshold of a New Decade, January 1959–December 1960* (Berkeley: University of California Press, 2005), 328, 357.

11. Baldwin, *There Is a Balm in Gilead*, 317–21.

12. Ibid.; John Hope Franklin, ed., *The Souls of Black Folk in Three Negro Classics* (New York: Avon, 1965 [1903]), 342; James Weldon Johnson, *God's Trombones: Seven Negro Sermons in Verse* (New York: Viking, 1977 [1927]), 2; Sterling Stuckey, *Slave Culture: Nationalist Theory and the Foundations of Black America* (New York: Oxford University Press, 1987), 255, 257; and Lewis V. Baldwin, "The Minister as Preacher, Pastor, and Prophet: The Thinking of Martin Luther King, Jr.," *American Baptist Quarterly* 7, no. 2 (June 1988): 84–85.

13. Here King's role once again recalls that of the slave priest who, according to Du Bois, functioned as "the interpreter of the Unknown, the comforter of the sorrowing, the supernatural avenger of wrong, and the one who rudely but picturesquely expressed the longing, disappointment, and resentment of a stolen and oppressed people." See Franklin, ed., *The Souls of Black Folk in Three Negro Classics*, 342; Baldwin, *There Is a Balm in Gilead*, 317–18; Baldwin, "The Minister as Preacher, Pastor, and Prophet," 84–85; and Stuckey, *Slave Culture*, 255, 257.

14. Clayborne Carson et al., eds., *The Papers of Martin Luther King, Jr.*, vol. 6: *Advocate of the Social Gospel, September 1948–March 1963* (Berkeley: University of California Press, 2007), 223–24.

15. Ibid.; and Baldwin, ed., *Never Alone*, ix–x.

16. Baldwin, ed., *Never Alone*, ix–x.

17. Carson et al., eds., *Papers of Martin Luther King, Jr.*, 6:223–24.

18. King, *Stride toward Freedom*, 178; and Baldwin, *There Is a Balm in Gilead*, 192.

19. Clayborne Carson et al., eds., *The Papers of Martin Luther King, Jr.*, vol. 1: *Called to Serve, January 1929–June 1951* (Berkeley: University of California Press, 1992), 189–94; and Carson et al., eds., *Papers of Martin Luther King, Jr.*, 6:275–92; Clayborne Carson et al., eds., *The Papers of Martin Luther King, Jr.*, vol. 2: *Rediscovering Precious Values, July 1951–November 1955* (Berkeley: University of California Press, 1994), 170, 207; and Clayborne Carson et al., eds., *The Papers of Martin Luther King, Jr.*, vol. 3: *Birth of a New Age, December 1955–December 1956* (Berkeley: University of California Press, 1997), 208.

20. Carson et al., eds., *Papers of Martin Luther King, Jr.*, 6:223–24, 262–70; and Carson et al., eds., *Papers of Martin Luther King, Jr.*, 5:166–67.

21. This is determined best by a careful reading of King's pastoral prayers, as they appear in various published and unpublished King documents. See Carson et al., eds., *Papers of Martin Luther King, Jr.*, 2:494; Carson et al., eds., *Papers of Martin Luther King, Jr.*, 3:74, 240, 267, 346, 361; Carson et al., eds., *Papers of Martin Luther King, Jr.*, 4:86, 151, 166–67; and Baldwin, ed., *Never Alone*, 13–20.

22. King viewed humans as worshiping creatures by nature, and this meant "seeing God high and lifted high," not only in the sacramental life of the church but in the activity of prayer as well. At the same time, he cautioned that God is never "placated by pious observances," which means that worship must always be taken seriously, regardless of the context in which it occurs. See Carson et al., eds., *Papers of Martin Luther King, Jr.*, 6:350–51. Also see King's pastoral prayers in Baldwin, ed., *Never Alone*, 13–20.

23. As noted earlier, this was also the case with King's sermons, which were always preceded by preparatory prayer. See Mervyn A. Warren, *King Came Preaching: The Pulpit Power of Dr. Martin Luther King Jr.* (Downers Grove, Ill.: InterVarsity, 2001), 158.

24. Vaughn and Wills, eds., *Reflections on Our Pastor*, 19, 55, 65, 100, 103.

25. This was King's way of saying that he was particularly devoted to what Jesus called "the least of these." See Martin Luther King Jr., "A Speech: Selma March," unpublished version (March 9, 1965), The Library

and Archives of the Martin Luther King Jr. Center for Nonviolent Social Change, Atlanta, Georgia, 1.

26. Carson et al., eds., *Papers of Martin Luther King, Jr.*, 2:287.

27. In this sense, King was very much in the tradition of his father and generations of black pastors who preceded him. But King was more apt than many black preachers in his time to acknowledge that his authority as pastor was also "humanly conferred," which means that he did not view that authority in dictatorial or autocratic terms. He understood that all too many pastors in black churches viewed themselves, first and foremost, as bosses of their parishioners and not so much as their servants. The tone of King's pastoral prayers reflected his sense of himself as the servant of his parishioners. See ibid.; and Baldwin, ed., *Never Alone*, 13–20.

28. Unlike so many black and white pastors in his time, King stressed the importance of having an intellectual understanding of the Christian faith. He categorically rejected all claims concerning the incompatibility of genuine spirituality and strong intellectual ability, and prayer would have come up in his own talks to the congregation and during the annual lecture series he started at the Dexter Avenue Baptist Church upon his arrival in 1954. Great pastors and intellectuals such as J. Pius Barbour, Samuel D. Proctor, Benjamin E. Mays, and Howard Thurman were among the "best minds" King invited to Dexter to talk about "some of the major doctrines and issues of the Christian faith." See Vaughn and Wills, eds., *Reflections on Our Pastor*, 26, 39; and Carson et al., eds., *Papers of Martin Luther King, Jr.*, 2:32, 45.

29. Philip Lenud, King's friend at Morehouse College and roommate in Boston, says that King himself "didn't dwell too much on metaphysics, that he was concerned with the pragmatics of existence, and the relationship of people with God in the valley." See Lewis V. Baldwin, private interview with Philip Lenud, Nashville, Tennessee (April 7, 1987); and Baldwin, *There Is a Balm in Gilead*, 300–301.

30. Carson et al., eds., *Papers of Martin Luther King, Jr.*, 6:223–25, 590–91.

31. Ibid., 180–81, 586–87.

32. Carson et al., eds., *Papers of Martin Luther King, Jr.*, 6:182–83, 225–28, 243–46, 275–83, 590–91.

33. Ibid., 243–46; and Baldwin, ed., *Never Alone*, 15–20.

34. Carson et al., eds., *Papers of Martin Luther King, Jr.*, 6:184–87, 249–50; and Baldwin, ed., *Never Alone*, 15–20.

35. King developed the concept of "the true *ekklesia*," which captured the ecclesial ideal for him, in his "Letter from the Birmingham City Jail" (1963). Here he was thinking of the early, apostolic church and its strict discipline of devotion, which, of course, included the life of prayer. The early church modeled what King hoped to see in the church of his own time, not only from the standpoint of the disciplined devotional life, but in terms of it nonconformist posture and its healthy tension with the state. See Martin Luther King Jr., *Why We Can't Wait* (New York: New American Library, 1964), 92; idem, *Strength to Love*, 78–79; idem, "What are Your New Year's Resolutions?" unpublished version of a statement, New York (January 7, 1968), King Center Library and Archives, 3; idem, "Transformed Nonconformist," unpublished version of sermon, Ebenezer Baptist Church, Atlanta, Georgia (January 16, 1966), King Center Library and Archives, 9–10; and idem, "Advice for Living," *Ebony* 12, no. 12 (October 1957): 53.

36. King, *Stride toward Freedom*, 178; Carson et al., eds., *Papers of Martin Luther King, Jr.*, 4:241, 311; and Vaughn and Wills, eds., *Reflections on Our Pastor*, 19, 65.

37. Carson et al., *The Papers of Martin Luther King, Jr.*, 6:91, 590–91; King, *Strength to Love*, 131–33, 155; and Martin Luther King Jr., *The Trumpet of Conscience* (New York: Harper & Row, 1989 [1967]), 59.

38. Carson et al., eds., *The Papers of Martin Luther King, Jr.*, 6:590–91.

39. "An Interview with Martin Luther King, Jr.," unpublished version prepared for *Redbook Magazine*, New York (November 5, 1964), King Center Library and Archives, 3; Carson et al., eds., *Papers of Martin Luther King, Jr.*, 6:471–72; Martin Luther King Jr. to Dr. Harold E. Fey, unpublished version of a letter (June 23, 1962), King Center Library and Archives, 3; Martin Luther King Jr., "Advice for Living," *Ebony* 13, no. 11 (September 1958): 68; Martin Luther King Jr. to Mr. M. Bernard Resnikoff, unpublished version of a letter (September 17, 1961), King Center Library and Archives, 1; and Lewis V. Baldwin and Amiri YaSin

Al-Hadid, *Between Cross and Crescent: Christian and Muslim Perspectives on Malcolm and Martin* (Gainesville: University Press of Florida, 2002), 116.

40. Carson et al., eds., *The Papers of Martin Luther King, Jr.*, 6:223, 294.

41. Ibid., 350.

42. Ibid.; Carson et al., eds., *Papers of Martin Luther God, Jr.*, 4:471–72; and King to Fey (June 23, 1962), 3–4.

43. Shelp and Sunderland, eds., *The Pastor as Prophet*, 15; and Baldwin, *There Is a Balm in Gilead*, 314–15.

44. From the beginning of the Montgomery bus boycott in December, 1955, King, as president of the Montgomery Improvement Association (MIA), was forced to either surrender or limit some of his pastoral duties, such as serving holy communion and visiting with and praying for the sick. Increasingly, his pastoral responsibilities at Dexter were passed on to his assistant ministers and visiting preachers. Also, King became more and more frustrated with his inability to reconcile his obligations as a full-time senior pastor with his broader commitments as a civil rights leader. In view of King's own comments on the matter, one would have to question Robert Franklin's claim that King did not allow "his public visibility to compromise his pastoral duties." See Carson et al., eds., *Papers of Martin Luther King, Jr.*, 5:328–32, 341–43, 351–57; Zelia S. Evans and J. T. Alexander, eds., *The Dexter Avenue Baptist Church, 1877–1977* (Montgomery: The Dexter Avenue Baptist Church, 1978), 141; "A Response to Martin Luther King, Jr.'s Announcement that He is Moving from Dexter to Atlanta," unpublished statement (November 29, 1959), King Center Library and Archives, 1–2; Vaughn and Wills, eds., *Reflections on Our Pastor*, 20, 27; Baldwin, *There Is a Balm in Gilead*, 194–95; Robert M. Franklin, "The Safest Place on Earth: The Culture of Black Congregations," in *American Congregations: New Perspectives in the Study of Congregations*, ed. James Wind and James W. Lewis (Chicago: University of Chicago Press, 1994), 2:269; Martin Luther King Jr., "Some Things We Must Do," unpublished version of speech (December 5, 1957), King Center Library and Archives, 2; and "King Calls Visit 'Gratifying Day,'" *Frontier Post*, Athens, Ohio (January 1, 1960), 4.

45. Carson et al., eds., *Papers of Martin Luther King, Jr.*, 5:323–24, 326; and Martin Luther King Jr., "Preaching Schedule for Ebenezer from July, 1962 through August, 1963," unpublished version of document (1962), King Center Library and Archives, 1–7.

46. King Jr. reported that when he arrived in Montgomery, Dexter Avenue Baptist Church was known as "the big folks church," the type of congregation that catered "only to a certain class." King sought to change that image with some success, but there remained obvious differences between Dexter and Ebenezer. See King, *Stride toward Freedom*, 25; and Lewis V. Baldwin, private interviews with Ralph D. Abernathy, Atlanta, Georgia (March 17, 1987; May 7, 1987).

47. Baldwin interview with Abernathy (May 7, 1987).

48. Martin Luther King Jr. to the Reverend W. H. McKinney (March 31, 1960), King Center Library and Archives, 1; Martin Luther King Jr. to Mrs. Wayne A. Dockhorn (September 29, 1960), King Center Library and Archives, 1; and Baldwin, *There Is a Balm in Gilead*, 195.

49. Support for these claims and conclusions is provided in King's pastoral prayers. See Baldwin, ed., *Never Alone*, 15–20. Also see James M. Washington, ed., *A Testament of Hope: The Essential Writings and Speeches of Martin Luther King, Jr.* (New York: HarperCollins, 1991), 41–42.

50. Gaylord Noyce has advanced this view, and I am indebted to him for much of this insight. See Noyce, *The Art of Pastoral Conversation*, 112.

51. Baldwin, ed., *Never Alone*, 15–20.

52. Ibid.

5| SPIRITS SOARING UPWARD

1. John Bartlett, *The Shorter Bartlett's Familiar Quotations: A Collection of Passages, Phrases, and Proverbs Traced to Their Sources in Ancient and Modern Literature*, ed. Christopher Morley (New York: Pocket, 1964), 405.

2. James M. Washington, ed., *Conversations with God: Two Centuries of Prayers by African Americans* (New York: HarperCollins, 1994), 39.

NOTES

139

3. Clayborne Carson, ed., *The Autobiography of Martin Luther King, Jr.* (New York: Warner, 1998), 105.

4. *Standing in the Need of Prayer: A Celebration of Black Prayer* (New York: Free, 2003), x–xii; Harold A. Carter, *The Prayer Tradition of Black People* (Valley Forge, Pa.: Judson, 1976), 20–21, 65–67, 94, 106–13, 129–30; Martin Luther King Jr., *Strength to Love* (Philadelphia: Fortress Press, 1981 [1963]), 131–33, 155; O. Richard Bowyer et al., *Prayer in the Black Tradition* (Nashville: Upper Room, 1986), 64–66; Harold A. Carter, "The Living Legacy of Dr. Martin Luther King, Jr. as Seen through the Streams of Prayer," in *No Other Help I Know: Sermons on Prayer and Spirituality*, ed. J. Alfred Smith Sr. (Valley Forge, Pa.: Judson, 1996), 11; and Mervyn A. Warren, *King Came Preaching: The Pulpit Power of Dr. Martin Luther King Jr.* (Downers Grove, Ill.: InterVarsity, 2001), 40, 136, 158.

5. King also referred to the civil rights movement as "a Christian social movement," "a reform movement," "a movement of Christian nonviolent reform," "the Christian social struggle," and a crusade rooted in "spiritual and moral forces." He always understood the movement in spiritual as well as social terms, and prayer was as important for him as creative nonviolent activism. See James M. Washington, ed., *A Testament of Hope: The Essential Writings and Speeches of Martin Luther King, Jr.* (New York: HarperCollins, 1991), 84; Martin Luther King, Jr. to David C. Dautzer, unpublished version of a letter (May 9, 1961), The Library and Archives of the Martin Luther King Jr. Center for Nonviolent Social Change, Atlanta, Georgia, 1; Martin Luther King Jr. to Truman Douglass, unpublished version of a letter (June 28, 1965), King Center Library and Archives, 2; Martin Luther King Jr., "An Ambitious Dream Confronts Reality," unpublished version of an essay written for *New York Amsterdam News*, New York (ca. June 23, 1965), King Center Library and Archives, 1; and Lewis V. Baldwin, *The Voice of Conscience: The Church in the Mind of Martin Luther King Jr.*, unpublished version of manuscript (2009), author's files, chapt. 3, 62–63n8.

6. Lewis V. Baldwin, ed., *Never Alone: The Prayers of Martin Luther King Jr.*, unpublished manuscript (2007), author's files, v.

7. Martin Luther King Jr., *Stride toward Freedom: The Montgomery Story* (New York: Harper & Row, 1958), 59–63; and Washington, ed.,

A Testament of Hope, 434–36. Harold Carter convincingly argues, "The whole philosophy of nonviolence, based on the love ethic of Jesus Christ, became real to King" in that "moment of prayer!" Carter goes on to declare that King "credited much of his strength during those early days to the ever-fresh stream of prayer." See Carter, *The Prayer Tradition of Black People*, 106–7. Interestingly enough, this very first mass meeting speech by King contained prayer lines, as he asked God to help him and the Negroes of Montgomery to "inject new meaning into the veins" of history and civilization "before it is too late." See Clayborne Carson et al., eds., *The Papers of Martin Luther King, Jr.*, vol. 3: *Birth of a New Age, December 1955–December 1956* (Berkeley: University of California Press, 1997), 74.

8. Baldwin, ed., *Never Alone*, vi.

9. King, *Stride toward Freedom*, 134–35; Clayborne Carson and Peter Holloran, eds., *A Knock at Midnight: Inspiration from the Great Sermons of Reverend Martin Luther King, Jr.* (New York: Warner, 1998), 159–62; Bowyer et al., *Prayer in the Black Tradition*, 65–66; and Lewis V. Baldwin, *There Is a Balm in Gilead: The Cultural Roots of Martin Luther King, Jr.* (Minneapolis: Fortress Press, 1991), 187–189.

10. Mervyn Warren calls this King's "prayer of relinquishment." One might safely contend that King found relief in "a personal, existential appropriation of black faith," which included fervent but secret communion with the deity. See King, *Stride toward Freedom*, 134–35; Carson and Holloran, eds., *A Knock at Midnight*, 159–62; Warren, *King Came Preaching*, 40; Alex Ayres, ed., *The Wisdom of Martin Luther King, Jr.: An A-to-Z Guide to the Ideas and Ideals of the Great Civil Rights Leader* (New York: Penguin, 1993), 183–84; and Baldwin, *There Is a Balm in Gilead*, 187–89.

11. Carter, *Prayer Tradition of Black People*, 106–9; Bowyer et al., *Prayer in the Black Tradition*, 65–66; Warren, *King Came Preaching*, 40–41, 136, 158; and Wally G. Vaughn and Richard W. Wills, eds., *Reflections on Our Pastor: Dr. Martin Luther King, Jr., at Dexter Avenue Baptist Church, 1954–1960* (Dover, Mass.: Majority, 1999), 122.

12. Warren, *King Came Preaching*, 40–41; Carter, *Prayer Tradition of Black People*, 108–9; and Baldwin, *There Is a Balm in Gilead*, 187–90.

13. King, *Stride toward Freedom*, 88, 137–138, 178; Carter, *Prayer Tradition of Black People*, 20–21, 65–67, 94, 106–10; King, *Strength to Love*, 131–33, 155; Washington, ed., *A Testament of Hope*, 84; and Martin Luther King Jr., *Why We Can't Wait* (New York: New American Library, 1964), 61.

14. King, *Stride toward Freedom*, 178; Vaughn and Wills, eds., *Reflections on Our Pastor*, 19, 103; and Carson, ed., *The Autobiography of Martin Luther King, Jr.*, 102.

15. Carson et al., eds., *Papers of Martin Luther King, Jr.*, 3:69–70, 85–86, 150–51, 231, 369–70; and King, *Stride toward Freedom*, 88.

16. Carson et al., eds., *Papers of Martin Luther King, Jr.*, 3:231; and King, *Stride toward Freedom*, 73, 169.

17. Carson et al., eds., *Papers of Martin Luther King, Jr.*, 3:151. One of King's former members at the Dexter Avenue Baptist Church reported that Lambert was "some kind of preacher" and that King "was crazy about him." But King sometimes found the comical side and laughed at preachers, including himself, and this was never meant to trivialize the preacher's significance as an artist and as a fashioner of culture. Coretta King, the wife of the civil rights leader, declares that King sometimes found humor "In the midst of the most serious times" and "even the most difficult situations." See Vaughn and Wills, eds., *Reflections on Our Pastor*, 8; Baldwin, *There Is a Balm in Gilead*, 306–10; and Coretta Scott King, *My Life with Martin Luther King, Jr.* (New York: Henry Holt, 1993 [1969]), 89.

18. King described Graetz as the "boyish-looking white minister of the Negro Trinity Lutheran Church," who stood as a reminder that there were whites in Montgomery who were applying the teachings and values of Christianity in their daily lives. See King, *Stride toward Freedom*, 66–67, 87–88; King, *My Life with Martin Luther King, Jr.*, 128, 131, 136; and Lewis V. Baldwin, private interview with Robert S. Graetz, Cincinnati, Ohio (July 26, 1988).

19. The Associated Press, unfamiliar with the power of the black worship experience, erroneously reported that King collapsed on this occasion. The civil rights leader received a number of telephone calls and letters from relatives and concerned citizens, inquiring about his

condition and offering prayer and words of comfort and hope. In any case, King's own account of what happened supports Harold Carter's claim that "the sustaining power of prayer was an invaluable anchor when physical violence exploded" in Montgomery. See King, *Stride toward Freedom*, 177–78; Carson, ed., *The Autobiography of Martin Luther King, Jr.*, 102; and Clayborne Carson et al., eds., *The Papers of Martin Luther King, Jr.*, vol. 4: *Symbol of the Movement, January 1957–December 1958* (Berkeley: University of California Press, 2000), 113.

20. King, *Stride toward Freedom*, 177–78; Vaughn and Wills, eds., *Reflections on Our Pastor*, 80 and 121–22; and Carson, ed., *Autobiography of Martin Luther King, Jr.*, 102.

21. Carson et al., eds., *Papers of Martin Luther King, Jr.*, 3:267, 328, 336, 346, 361, 373, 461, 477–78; Carson et al., eds., *Papers of Martin Luther King, Jr.*, 4:122–23, 151, 166–67, 340; Clayborne Carson et al., eds., *The Papers of Martin Luther King, Jr.*, vol. 6: *Advocate of the Social Gospel, September 1948–March 1963* (Berkeley: University of California Press, 2007), 267; Washington, ed., *A Testament of Hope*, 84; and Baldwin, ed., *Never Alone*, 43–59.

22. Carson et al., eds., *Papers of Martin Luther King, Jr.*, 4:255; and Carter, *Prayer Tradition of Black People*, 94, 106–10.

23. King said this was the prayer he prayed "to God every day." He also noted that Montgomery had "several marvelous leaders" and that his own absence did not in any way "impede the program of our movement." See Carson et al., eds., *Papers of Martin Luther King, Jr.*, 4:255, 505; and Carson, ed., *The Autobiography of Martin Luther King, Jr.*, 105.

24. Carson et al., eds., *Papers of Martin Luther King, Jr.*, 4:86, 178, 190, 211, 340; and Carson et al., eds., *Papers of Martin Luther King, Jr.*, 3:336.

25. Carson et al., eds., *Papers of Martin Luther King, Jr.*, 4:241–42, 540; and Carson et al., eds., *Papers of Martin Luther King, Jr.*, 6:265, 267, 270.

26. Martin Luther King Jr. to Dr. J. Ellis, unpublished version of a letter (February 6, 1960), The Martin Luther King Jr. Papers, Special Collections, Mugar Memorial Library, Boston University, Boston, Massachusetts, 1–2; Adam Fairclough, "The Southern Christian Leadership

Conference and the Second Reconstruction, 1957–1973," *The Southern Atlantic Quarterly* 8, no. 2 (Spring 1981): 178; Adam Fairclough, *To Redeem the Soul of America: The Southern Christian Leadership Conference and Martin Luther King, Jr.* (Athens: University of Georgia Press, 1987), 1–2; Carson et al., eds., *Papers of Martin Luther King, Jr.*, 4:151, 505; King, *Stride toward Freedom*, 137–38; Vaughn and Wills, eds., *Reflections on Our Pastor*, 109; Washington, ed., *A Testament of Hope*, 84; and Baldwin, *There Is a Balm in Gilead*, 67, 86, 192–93.

27. Carson et al., eds., *Papers of Martin Luther King, Jr.*, 4:151–53, 540; Clayborne Carson et al., eds., *The Papers of Martin Luther King, Jr.*, vol. 5: *Threshold of a New Decade, January 1959–December 1960* (Berkeley: University of California Press, 2005), 370; Carson et al., eds., *Papers of Martin Luther King, Jr.*, 3:327, 452, 459; and Carson et al., eds., *Papers of Martin Luther King, Jr.*, 6:269, 307.

28. Carson et al., eds., *Papers of Martin Luther King, Jr.*, 6:279–81.

29. Ibid., 299–301.

30. It is said that the Prayer Pilgrimage to the Lincoln Memorial in May, 1957, actually moved King "beyond being a nationally and internationally known preacher to being the number one spokesman for the Negro." See Warren, *King Came Preaching*, 41.

31. King, *Stride toward Freedom*, 87–88; Carson, ed., *The Autobiography of Martin Luther King, Jr.*, 102, 105; and Carson et al., eds., *Papers of Martin Luther King, Jr.*, 3:240, 267, 328.

32. Carson et al., eds., *Papers of Martin Luther King, Jr.*, 3:279–80; Washington, ed., *A Testament of Hope*, 84; Carson et al., eds., *Papers of Martin Luther King, Jr.*, 4:113, 151, 208, 396; and Vaughn and Wills, eds., *Reflections on Our Pastor*, 135.

33. Warren, *King Came Preaching*, 40, 136, 158.

34. Carter, *The Prayer Tradition of Black People*, 94.

35. Nathan I. Huggins, "Martin Luther King, Jr.: Charisma and Leadership," *Journal of American History* 74, no. 2 (September 1987): 480–81; Baldwin, *There Is a Balm in Gilead*, 186; and Carter, *Prayer Tradition of Black People*, 65–67.

36. Ibid., 106; Baldwin, ed., *Never Alone*, xiii; and King, *Why We Can't Wait*, 61.

37. Carter's view of prayer as "a source of inner release and personal fulfillment" and Mervyn Warren's idea of prayer as "a necessary Christian process" are equally significant for understanding the role that prayer played in all King-led civil rights campaigns. See Carter, *Prayer Tradition of Black People*, 21, 110; and Warren, *King Came Preaching*, 137.

38. "Why Our Prayer Vigil," unpublished version of a Group Statement of the Negotiating Committee of the Albany Movement and Its Chief Consultants, Dr. Martin Luther King Jr. and Ralph Abernathy (1962), King Center Library and Archives, 1–2.

39. Martin Luther King Jr., " Message from Jail," unpublished version, Albany, Georgia (1962), King Center Library and Archives, 1–2.

40. William D. Watley, *Roots of Resistance: The Nonviolent Ethic of Martin Luther King, Jr.* (Valley Forge, Pa.: Judson, 1985), 65; Carter, *The Prayer Tradition of Black People*, 110; Charles Osborne, ed., *I Have a Dream* (New York: Time-Life Books, 1968), 30–31; and John J. Ansbro, *Martin Luther King, Jr.: Nonviolent Strategies and Tactics for Social Change* (Lanham, Md.: Madison, 2000 [1982]), 316n116.

41. Carson, ed., *The Autobiography of Martin Luther King, Jr.*, 154, 158–159, 161; and King, *Why We Can't Wait*, 69, 75.

42. Carter, *The Prayer Tradition of Black People*, 111; King, *Why We Can't Wait*, 61; and Carson, *The Autobiography of Martin Luther King, Jr.*, 178, 180, 183.

43. Carter, *Prayer Tradition of Black People*, 111; and Harold A. Carter, a personal interview with Wyatt Tee Walker, Rochester, New York (July 20, 1974), author's files.

44. Warren, *King Came Preaching*, 136, 158; and letter from Wyatt Tee Walker to Lewis V. Baldwin (April 30, 2009).

45. Howard Thurman, the black theologian and philosopher of religion, may have had a greater influence on King at this level than we have been led to believe. From the time of his graduate studies at Boston University and perhaps earlier, King was exposed to Thurman's sermons and talks on the phenomenon of the inner spiritual life. See Lewis V. Baldwin, private interview with Philip Lenud, Nashville, Tennessee (April 7, 1987); and Baldwin, *There Is a Balm in Gilead*, 146, 300–301.

46. Carson, ed., *The Autobiography of Martin Luther King, Jr.*, 58–59, 105; King, *Stride toward Freedom*, 59–63; Carson and Holloran, eds., *A Knock at Midnight*, 160–64, 186; letter from Wyatt Tee Walker to Lewis V. Baldwin (April 30, 2009); Warren, *King Came Preaching*, 136, 158; Carter, *The Prayer Tradition of Black People*, 65–67; *Standing in the Need of Prayer*, x; and Baldwin, ed., *Never Alone*, 39–59.

47. Gayraud Wilmore describes King's role in these terms, suggesting that his priestly role was not confined to the traditional church or to his activities as a pastor. See Choan-seng Song and Gayraud S. Wilmore, *Asians and Blacks: Joseph Cook Memorial Lectures*, Sixth Series (Spring 1972), Part 2, 70; and Baldwin, *There Is a Balm in Gilead*, 317–22.

48. Washington, ed., *A Testament of Hope*, 221–23; Lewis V. Baldwin, *To Make the Wounded Whole: The Cultural Legacy of Martin Luther King, Jr.* (Minneapolis: Fortress Press, 1992), 84; and Baldwin, *There Is a Balm in Gilead*, 321–22.

49. Carter, *Prayer Tradition of Black People*, 113.

50. King's fascination with massive prayer pilgrimages actually dated back to the Montgomery bus boycott. In May, 1956, he delivered a sermon at a "Service of Prayer and Thanksgiving" at The Cathedral of St. John the Divine, the headquarters of the Episcopal diocese for the state of New York, commemorating the second anniversary of the Supreme Court decision in Brown vs. Board of Education. In April, 1958, King gave a statement at a prayer pilgrimage in Montgomery, protesting the electrocution of Jeremiah Reeves, who was believed to be innocent of the charge of raping a white woman. Massive gatherings in various cities, devoted to the phenomenon of prayer, "provided a national and international platform for King to call the nation to repentance and sound justice." See Carson et al., eds., *Papers of Martin Luther King, Jr.*, 3:256–62; Carson et al., eds., *Papers of Martin Luther King, Jr.*, 4:151–53, 208–15, 396–98; King, *Stride toward Freedom*, 31–32; and Carter, *The Prayer Tradition of Black People*, 110, 112.

51. Carson, ed., *The Autobiography of Martin Luther King, Jr.*, 222. From the time of his activities in Montgomery, King had been mindful of the tremendous potential of interfaith prayer. See Carson et al., eds., *Papers of Martin Luther King, Jr.*, 6:350.

52. Fairclough, *To Redeem the Soul of America*, 181–91; and Washington, ed., *A Testament of Hope*, 351–52. L. Harold DeWolf, King's former professor, spoke of having had the "privilege" to "agonize and pray with" the civil rights leader "in the midst of the worst violence at St. Augustine." See L. Harold DeWolf, "Funeral Tribute to Martin Luther King, Jr.," unpublished version, Ebenezer Baptist Church, Atlanta, Georgia (April 9, 1968), King Center Library and Archives, 1.

53. Baldwin, *There Is a Balm in Gilead*, 204–5; Charles E. Fager, *Selma, 1965: The March That Changed the South* (Boston: Beacon, 1985), 8, 40, 116; and Donzaleigh Abernathy, *Partners to History: Martin Luther King, Jr., Ralph Abernathy, and the Civil Rights Movement* (New York: Crown, 2003), 154.

54. King spoke of Jackson, Reeb, and Liuzzo as "martyrs of the faith." See Sophie Spencer-Wood, ed., *Freedom: A Photographic History of the African American Struggle* (New York: Phaidon, n.d.), 365; Martin Luther King Jr., "Statement Regarding the Death of Rev. James Reeb," unpublished version (March 11, 1965), King Center Library and Archives, 1–6; Martin Luther King Jr., "Tribute to James Reeb," unpublished version, Montgomery, Alabama (March 16, 1965), King Center Library and Archives, 1; Carson, ed., *The Autobiography of Martin Luther King, Jr.*, 282–83, 289; and Washington, ed., *A Testament of Hope*, 56.

55. Carson, ed., *The Autobiography of Martin Luther King, Jr.*, 270, 282–83, 287, 289, 294, 323–24.

56. Martin Luther King Jr., "A Speech: Selma March," unpublished version (March 9, 1965), King Center Library and Archives, 1. This speech consists of a short prayer, versions of which were undoubtedly recited in the streets and in church settings in various small towns in the South. The prayer circle stood out as a central feature of the Selma campaign, thus recalling its significance generations earlier at Big August Quarterly celebrations in Delaware, in Gullah culture in the Georgia–South Carolina sea coast areas, and in slave cultures throughout the southern United States, Latin America, and the Caribbean. See Baldwin, ed., *Never Alone*, 55–56; Lewis V. Baldwin, *"Invisible" Strands in African Methodism: A History of the African Union Methodist Protestant and Union American Methodist Episcopal Churches, 1805–1980* (Metuchen, N.J.: Scarecrow,

1983), 137–40; Lewis V. Baldwin, *The Mark of a Man: Peter Spencer and the African Union Methodist Tradition* (Lanham, Md.: University Press of America, 1987), 24–25; Margaret Washington Creel, *"A Peculiar People": Slave Religion and Community-Culture Among the Gullahs* (New York: New York University Press, 1988), 297–99; Albert J. Raboteau, *Slave Religion: The "Invisible Institution" in the Antebellum South* (New York: Oxford University Press, 2004), 215–16; and William S. Pollitzer, *The Gullah People and Their African Heritage* (Athens: University of Georgia Press, 1999), 151.

57. Martin Luther King Jr., "A Prayer for Chicago," *Newsletter of the Southern Christian Leadership Conference (SCLC)* 3, no. 1 (January–February 1966): 2; and Baldwin, ed., *Never Alone*, 56–58.

58. King, "A Prayer for Chicago," 2; Martin Luther King Jr., "A Prayer at the March on Chicago," unpublished version, Chicago, Illinois (July 26, 1965), King Center Library and Archives, 1–7; Martin Luther King Jr., "A Prayer for Chicago," *Chicago Defender* (April 16, 1966), 10; and Baldwin, ed., *Never Alone*, 56–58.

59. Carter, *The Prayer Tradition of Black People*, 106.

60. King, *Strength to Love*, 132.

61. *Standing in the Need of Prayer*, x.

62. Carson et al., eds., *Papers of Martin Luther King, Jr.*, 3:256–62; Carson et al., eds., *Papers of Martin Luther King, Jr.*, 4:14–15, 43, 151–53, 197–98; Carter, *The Prayer Tradition of Black People*, 112; Warren, *King Came Preaching*, 41; "Why Our Prayer Vigil," 1–2; Martin Luther King Jr., "First Ban of Selma March," unpublished version of prayer and statement, Selma, Alabama (March 1965), King Center Library and Archives, 1–2; idem, "Night Vigil," unpublished version of statement, Selma, Alabama (March 13, 1965), King Center Library and Archives, 1; idem, "The Terrible Cost of the Ballot," unpublished version of statement (September 1, 1962), King Center Library and Archives, 3; idem, "Message from Jail," 1–2; and Baldwin, ed., *Never Alone*, xii, 40. Interestingly enough, prayer vigils, like the call to prayer, prayer pilgrimages, and prayer meetings, are deeply rooted in the history of Christian activism. See David A. deSilva, *Praying with John Wesley* (Nashville: Discipleship Resources, 1989), 29.

63. King, *Why We Can't Wait*, 78; Carson et al., eds., *Papers of Martin Luther King, Jr.*, 5:393; Washington, ed., *A Testament of Hope*, 84, 290; and Carson, ed., *The Autobiography of Martin Luther King, Jr.*, 105, 189.

64. Baldwin, ed., *Never Alone*, 40–41.

65. Ibid., xi–xii, 41.

66. Ibid.; and Carson et al., eds., *Papers of Martin Luther King, Jr.*, 5:170.

67. Carson, ed., *The Autobiography of Martin Luther King, Jr.*, 77, 105; Carson et al., eds., *Papers of Martin Luther King, Jr.*, 4:255, 505; and Baldwin, *There Is a Balm in Gilead*, 328.

68. Carson et al., eds., *Papers of Martin Luther King, Jr.*, 3:74, 346; Carson et al., eds., *Papers of Martin Luther King, Jr.*, 4:166; and Baldwin, ed., *Never Alone*, 43–59.

69. John H. Cartwright, "Foundations of the Beloved Community," *Debate and Understanding: A Semestral Review of Black Americans' Political, Economic and Social Development* 1, no. 3 (Semester 2, 1977): 171–74; John H. Cartwright, ed., *Essays in Honor of Martin Luther King, Jr.* (Evanston, Ill.: Leiffer Bureau of Social and Religious Research, 1971), 9–10; Kenneth L. Smith and Ira G. Zepp Jr., *Search for the Beloved Community: The Thinking of Martin Luther King, Jr.* (Valley Forge, Pa.: Judson, 1998), 141–45; Lewis V. Baldwin, *Toward the Beloved Community: Martin Luther King, Jr., and South Africa* (Cleveland: Pilgrim, 1995), 2; and Ansbro, *Martin Luther King, Jr.*, 187–97. Kenneth Smith has suggested that for King, the ethical ideal of the beloved community translated, in sociopolitical and economic terms, into democratic socialism. See Kenneth L. Smith, "The Radicalization of Martin Luther King, Jr.: The Last Three Years," *Journal of Ecumenical Studies* 26, no. 2 (Spring 1989): 270–87.

70. Baldwin, ed., *Never Alone*, 43–59

71. King, *Strength to Love*, 131–33, 155; Carson, ed., *The Autobiography of Martin Luther King, Jr.*, 42–43, 77–78; *Standing in the Need of Prayer*, x; Bowyer et al., *Prayer in the Black Tradition*, 64–66; Washington, ed., *A Testament of Hope*, 84; and Warren, *King Came Preaching*, 40–41. King's accounts support Harold Carter's contention that the black prayer tradition "was an undergirder of the liberation efforts of Black people and the civil rights movement." See Carter, *The Prayer Tradition of Black People*, 20–21.

72. Carson et al., eds., *Papers of Martin Luther King, Jr.*, 5:281; Martin Luther King Jr., "A Speech," unpublished version delivered at a dinner honoring him as a Nobel Peace Prize recipient, Dinkler Plaza Hotel, Atlanta, Georgia (January 27, 1965), King Center Library and Archives, 16; and Baldwin, *There Is a Balm in Gilead*, 88.

73. Carson et al., eds., *Papers of Martin Luther King, Jr.*, 6:350; Carson et al., eds., *Papers of Martin Luther King, Jr.*, 3:346; and Carson et al., eds., *Papers of Martin Luther King, Jr.*, 4:342–43.

74. King's movement prayers reflected this kind of confidence, especially during the last three years of his life, when he, after receiving the Nobel Peace Prize, felt the need to increasingly address world problems. His prayers, much like his sermons and mass meeting speeches, highlighted his vision of a globalized, interdependent, and interrelated world. See Baldwin, ed., *Never Alone*, 38, 58–59.

75. Baldwin, ed., *Never Alone*, 41; King, *Strength to Love*, 131–33, 155; and Carson et al., eds., *Papers of Martin Luther King, Jr.*, 6:590–91.

76. Baldwin, ed., *Never Alone*, xx; King, *Strength to Love*, 131–33; Ayres, ed., *The Wisdom of Martin Luther King, Jr.*, 184; and Carter, "The Living Legacy of Dr. Martin Luther King, Jr.," 11.

77. Albert J. Raboteau, "African-Americans, Exodus, and the American Israel," in *African-American Christianity: Essays in History*, ed. Paul E. Johnson, (Berkeley: University of California Press, 1994), 13.

78. King, *Strength to Love*, 132; Carson et al., eds., *Papers of Martin Luther King, Jr.*, 6:590–91; and Bowyer et al., *Prayer in the Black Tradition*, 64. On one occasion, King told a group that assembled to hear him speak: "But if you end up doing nothing but praying we will be living in segregation two hundred or three hundred years from now." See Martin Luther King Jr., "Answer to a Perplexing Question," unpublished version of a sermon, Atlanta, Georgia (March 3, 1963), King Center Library and Archives, 9–11; Carter, *The Prayer Tradition of Black people*, 65–66; and Carson et al., eds., *Papers of Martin Luther King, Jr.*, 6:590–91.

79. King, *Stride toward Freedom*, 36.

80. Martin Luther King Jr., *The Trumpet of Conscience* (New York: Harper & Row, 1987 [1967]), 59; King, *Strength to Love*, 131–32; and Bowyer et al., *Prayer in the Black Tradition*, 64–65.

81. Baldwin, *To Make the Wounded Whole*, 258; Martin Luther King Jr., *Where Do We Go from Here: Chaos or Community?* (Boston: Beacon, 1968), 186; and idem, *Strength to Love*, 132.

82. Baldwin, ed., *Never Alone*, xix.

83. King, *Strength to Love*, 131–32; idem, "Answer to a Perplexing Question," 9–11; Bowyer et al., *Prayer in the Black Tradition*, 64–65; and Carson et al., eds., *Papers of Martin Luther King, Jr.*, 6:369–370, 590–91.

84. Carter, *The Prayer Tradition of Black People*, 106.

85. King, *Strength to Love*, 100; idem, *Where Do We Go from Here?*, 178; idem, "A Cry of Hate or a Cry for Help?" unpublished version of statement (August 1965), King Center Library and Archives, 4; idem, "Revolution and Redemption," unpublished version of closing address at the European Baptist Assembly, Amsterdam, Holland (August 16, 1964), King Center Library and Archives, 9; and idem, "A Lecture," unpublished version, delivered under the auspices of The Federation Protestante de France Mutualite, Paris, France (October 24, 1965), King Center Library and Archives, 16.

86. King, *Where Do We Go from Here?*, 184, 188.

87. This was the motto of King's Southern Christian Leadership Conference (SCLC) from the time of its founding in 1957. King's prayerful mood leading up to the establishment of the organization was quite obvious, as he noted that blacks were "called upon to be God's suffering servants." Some of the prayers King delivered in that period were described as "emotional" and accompanied by calls for blacks to remain nonviolent and peaceful. See Baldwin, *There Is a Balm in Gilead*, 192, 235; Carson et al., eds., *Papers of Martin Luther King, Jr.*, 4:5, 94–96, 103–6, 109; and Washington, ed., *A Testament of Hope*, xix.

88. Washington, ed., *A Testament of Hope*, 41–42; King, *Strength to Love*, 110–14; and Carson, ed., *The Autobiography of Martin Luther King, Jr.*, 77–78.

6| TOWARD A HARMONIOUS WHOLE

1. John Barlett, *The Shorter Barlett's Familiar Quotations: A Collection of Passages, Phrases, and Proverbs Traced to Their Sources in Ancient*

and Modern Literature, ed. Christopher Morley (New York: Pocket, 1964), 250.

2. L. Harold DeWolf, "Funeral Tribute to Martin Luther King, Jr.," unpublished version, Ebenezer Baptist Church, Atlanta, Georgia (April 9, 1969), The Library and Archives of the Martin Luther King Jr. Center for Nonviolent Social Change, Atlanta, Georgia, 1.

3. Martin Luther King Jr., "Some Things We Must Do," unpublished version of an address, Montgomery, Alabama (December 5, 1957), King Center Library and Archives, 3.

4. Lerone Bennett Jr., *What Manner of Man: A Biography of Martin Luther King, Jr.* (New York: Pocket, 1968), 145; "Roundup: Foreign Tributes to Dr. King," *The Christian Century* 85, no. 19 (May 8, 1968): 629–30; and Lewis V. Baldwin, *To Make the Wounded Whole: The Cultural Legacy of Martin Luther King, Jr.* (Minneapolis: Fortress Press, 1992), 289.

5. Bennett, *What Manner of Man,* 146.

6. DeWolf, "Funeral Tribute to Martin Luther King, Jr.," 1.

7. Baldwin, *To Make the Wounded Whole,* 289–90.

8. Needless to say, answers to these questions are more accessible through a careful reading of King's own prayers. See Lewis V. Baldwin, ed., *Never Alone: The Prayers of Martin Luther King Jr.,* unpublished manuscript (2007), author's files, 1–59.

9. "Nashville to Mark National Day of Prayer," *The Tennessean* (May 2, 2009), 3B; Bob Smietana, "Prayers Fill Sommet Plaza: Event Resonates Amid Recession," *The Tennessean* (May 8, 2009), 1B, 10B; Bob Smietana, "Non-Christians Feel Left Out on Day of Prayer," *The Tennessean* (May 7, 2009), 1A, 10A; "Students, Not Schools, Must Control Prayer," *The Tennessean* (March 18, 2009), 10A; and K. Hollyn Hollman, "Columnist Misrepresents Religion Clauses," *The Tennessean* (March 14, 2009), 14A.

10. It is important to point out that "the White House is acting in a deliberately inclusive, interfaith way that seems to limit opposition." According to "Church-state experts," Obama's policy, which he "also followed while campaigning," is not really "illegal because the White House tells people who lead the prayers to be nonsectarian." Even so, concerns are being raised about the prayer policy. See Michelle Boorstein, "Obama

Raises Profile of Prayer," *The Tennessean* (March 11, 2009), 5A; and Nancy Gibbs and Michael Duffy, "Leveling the Praying Field: The Democratic Front Runners are Leading Their Party's Crusade to Win Over Religious Voters," *Time* (July 23, 2007), 28–34.

11. Smietana, "Prayers Fill Sommet Plaza," 1B.

12. Joseph L. Price, ed., *From Season to Season: Sports as American Religion* (Macon, Ga.: Mercer University Press, 2001), 16, 26; Nicole Young, "Prayer Signs OK in Some Schools: Rules in Other Districts Differ from Wilson's," *The Tennessean* (March 6, 2009), 2B; Clancy Hall, "Faith, Teaching are Inseparable," *The Tennessean* (March 18, 2009), 10A; Mike Organ, "Case Could Bar Coaches from Praying with Players," *The Tennessean* (February 24, 2009), 1A, 10A; and "Court Draws Line at Team Prayer," *The Tennessean* (March 18, 2009), 10A.

13. "World Day of Prayer," *The United Methodist Reporter: The Tennessee Conference* (March 6, 1998), 1.

14. Clayborne Carson et al., eds., *The Papers of Martin Luther King, Jr.*, vol. 6: *Advocate of the Social Gospel, September 1948–March 1963* (Berkeley: University of California Press, 2007), 590–91; Martin Luther King Jr., *Strength to Love* (Philadelphia: Fortress Press, 1981 [1963]), 131–33; and O. Richard Bowyer et al., *Prayer in the Black Tradition* (Nashville: Upper Room, 1986), 64–65.

15. Harold A. Carter, *The Prayer Tradition of Black People* (Valley Forge, Pa.: Judson, 1976), 65–66; Carson et al., eds., *Papers of Martin Luther King, Jr.*, 6:590; and Martin Luther King Jr., *Stride toward Freedom: The Montgomery Story* (New York: Harper & Row, 1958), 59.

16. Bonna Johnson, "Volunteers Pray for Tenn. Execs: Christian Chamber Adopts Top Employers," *The Tennessean* (April 15, 2009), B4, 7B; Smietana, "Prayers Fill Sommet Plaza," 1B, 10B; and Bob Smietana, "Prayer Centers Get More Job Pleas: Counselors Offer Hurting Callers Hope," *The Tennessean* (February 4, 2009), 1A, 12A.

17. Smietana, "Prayer Centers Get More Job Pleas," 1A, 12A; and "Prayer for Finances: It Works," e-mail from Judie Sanders to Lewis V. Baldwin and others (March 5, 2009), 1–6.

18. "Lott Carey Prayer Alert!: Earthquake in Italy," e-mail from Lott Carey International, Washington, D.C. (April 7, 2009), 1–2.

19. Ernesto Londono, "Separation Anxiety Rises in Sadr City," *The Tennessean* (May 19, 2009), 5A.

20. Claudia Pinto, "Meditation Eases Minds in These Troubled Times: More People Turn to Ancient Practice in Stressful Times," *The Tennessean* (March 17, 2009), 1D, 8D.

21. James M. Washington, ed., *A Testament of Hope: The Essential Writings and Speeches of Martin Luther King, Jr.* (New York: HarperCollins, 1991), 373. In referring to "the Radical Right," King actually had in mind political conservatives in the Republican Party and diehard segregationists from the South. At times, King spoke of "the fanaticism of the Right," bringing into focus its extreme views on issues like school prayer. See Martin Luther King Jr., "Address at the Southern Association of Political Scientists," unpublished version (November 13, 1964), King Center Library and Archives, 1–2; and Clayborne Carson et al., eds., *The Papers of Martin Luther King, Jr.*, vol. 4: *Symbol of the Movement, January 1957–December 1958* (Berkeley: University of California Press, 2000), 211.

22. Organ, "Case Could Bar Coaches from Praying with Players," 1A, 10A; Young, "Prayer Signs OK in Some Schools," 2B; Hall, "Faith, Teaching are Inseparable," 10A; "Court Draws Line at Team Prayer," 10A; Hollman, "Columnist Misrepresents Religion Clauses," 14A; "Students, Not Schools, Must Control Prayer," 10A; Jesse J. Holland, "Coach Loses Bid to Join Team in Pregame Prayer," *The Tennessean* (March 3, 2009), 4A; Jack Chapman, "God Doesn't Believe in Atheists: Letter to the Editor," *The Tennessean* (May 11, 2009), 7A; Nancy T. Ammerman, *Baptist Battles: Social Change and Religious Conflict in the Southern Baptist Convention* (New Brunswick, N.J.: Rutgers University Press, 1990), 55, 99, 240; James D. Hunter, *Culture Wars—The Struggle to Define America: Making Sense of the Battles Over the Family, Art, Education, Law, and Politics* (New York: Basic, 1991), 91, 198, 203–4, 264–65, 267–68, 277, 324; and Barry Hankins, *American Evangelicals: A Contemporary History of a Mainstream Religious Movement* (Lanham, Md.: Rowman & Littlefield, 2008), 144–45, 148.

23. But King held that "even the most devout atheist will at times cry out for the God that his theory denies." This was most certainly consistent with his belief that prayer is natural to the human spirit. See Carson et al., eds., *Papers of Martin Luther King, Jr.*, 6:590.

24. Washington, ed., *A Testament of Hope*, 373; and Lewis V. Baldwin et al., *The Legacy of Martin Luther King, Jr.: The Boundaries of Law, Politics, and Religion* (Notre Dame, Ind.: University of Notre Dame Press, 2002), 103–6. For brilliant insights into how King's ideas and movement contrast with the agenda and thrust of the religious and political Right in more recent times, see Daniel C. Maguire, *The New Subversives: Anti-Americanism of the Religious Right* (New York: Continuum, 1982), 39–42.

25. Carson et al., eds., *Papers of Martin Luther King, Jr.*, 6:97, 223, 590; and King, *Strength to Love*, 131–32, 155.

26. Carson et al., eds., *Papers of Martin Luther King, Jr.*, 6:350.

27. Ibid., 97, 203–4, 223–25, 350, 590–91

28. Ibid.; King, *Strength to Love*, 131–33, 155; idem, *Stride toward Freedom*, 59, 63; and Washington, ed., *A Testament of Hope*, 84.

29. King, *Strength to Love*, 147.

30. King, *Stride toward Freedom*, 59, 134–35; Clayborne Carson and Peter Holloran, eds., *A Knock at Midnight: Inspiration from the Great Sermons of Reverend Martin Luther King, Jr.* (New York: Warner, 1998), 160–62; Baldwin, ed., *Never Alone*, v–x; and letter from Wyatt Tee Walker to Lewis V. Baldwin (April 30, 2009).

31. Carson et al., eds., *Papers of Martin Luther King, Jr.*, 6:590–91; King, *Strength to Love*, 131–33; Bowyer et al., *Prayer in the Black Tradition*, 64–65; Martin Luther King Jr., *The Trumpet of Conscience* (New York: Harper & Row, 1987 [1967]), 59; and Harold A. Carter, "The Living Legacy of Dr. Martin Luther King, Jr., as Seen Through the Streams of Prayer," in *No Other Help I Know: Sermons on Prayer and Spirituality*, ed. J. Alfred Smith (Valley Forge, Pa.: Judson, 1996), 11.

32. Carson et al., eds., *Papers of Martin Luther King, Jr.*, 6:97, 203–4, 350–51, 590–91; Carson et al., eds., *Papers of Martin Luther King, Jr.*, 4:108, 342; Clayborne Carson et al., eds., *The Papers of Martin Luther King, Jr.*, vol. 1: *Called to Serve, January 1929–June 1951* (Berkeley: University of California Press, 1992), 191–92; Clayborne Carson et al., eds., *The Papers of Martin Luther King, Jr.*, vol. 5: *Threshold of a New Decade, January 1959–December 1960* (Berkeley: University of California Press, 2005), 166–67; and King, *Stride toward Freedom*, 137–38.

33. King spoke plainly to this as early as his student days. In a sermon called "Mastering Our Evil Selves, Mastering Ourselves," delivered at his home church in Atlanta, Georgia, in June, 1949, when he was still in seminary, King urged his listeners to master themselves by "developing a continuous prayer and devotional life." See Carson et al., eds., *Papers of Martin Luther King, Jr.*, 6:97.

34. King called this worshiping "Christ emotionally, but not morally." See ibid., 97, 231–34, 591; and Martin Luther King Jr., "A Knock at Midnight," unpublished version of sermon, All Saints Community Church, Los Angeles, California (June 25, 1967), King Center Library and Archives, 7–8. King used the story of the Pharisee and publican praying in the temple, in Luke 18:9-14, to illustrate his point about prayer as a lived experience and about achieving consistency between faith and practice. The Pharisee, says King, "confused ceremonial piety with genuine religious living." See Martin Luther King Jr., "Pharisee and Publican," unpublished version of sermon, Atlanta, Georgia (October 9, 1966), King Center Library and Archives, 2–3.

35. Carson et al., eds., *Papers of Martin Luther King, Jr.*, 6:591; and Baldwin, ed., *Never Alone*, 1–59.

36. "Obama Takes Leap of Faith," *The Tennessean* (February 14, 2009), 14A; Matthew Lee, "An Isolated Iran Gives U.S. Shot at Mideast Peace," *The Tennessean* (May 24, 2009), 1A, 14A; "Obama Pushes Israel on Settlement Issue," *The Tennessean* (May 29, 2009), 4A; Jeffrey Fleishman, "Muslim World Looks to Obama: Great Expectations Will Greet President's Speech in Mideast," *The Tennessean* (June 3, 2009), 1A; "Obama to Reach Out to Muslims in Speech," *The Tennessean* (May 29, 2009), 4A; "Will Obama Speech Bring Change to Muslim World?" *The Tennessean* (June 5, 2009), 13A; and Boorstein, "Obama Raises Profile of Prayer," 5A.

37. King saw this kind of an "alliance of conscience" as "a sign of the coming of the Kingdom." See Martin Luther King Jr., "An Address at the Synagogue Council of America," unpublished version (December 5, 1965), King Center Library and Archives, 2; James Hennesey, S.J., *American Catholics: A History of the Roman Catholic Community in the United States* (New York: Oxford University Press, 1983), 315; Martin Luther

King Jr., *Where Do We Go from Here: Chaos or Community?* (Boston: Beacon, 1968), 9; Martin Luther King Jr., "Closing Address," before the National Conference on Religion and Race, Chicago, Illinois (January 17, 1963), unpublished version, King Center Library and Archives, 2; Lewis V. Baldwin, *There Is a Balm in Gilead: The Cultural Roots of Martin Luther King, Jr.* (Minneapolis: Fortress Press, 1991), 204; Charles E. Fager, *Selma, 1965: The March That Changed the South* (Boston: Beacon, 1985), 8, 40, 116; and Sheyann Webb and Rachel West Nelson, *Selma, Lord, Selma: Girlhood Memories of the Civil Rights Days as Told to Frank Sikora* (Tuscaloosa: University of Alabama Press, 1997), 11, 15, 17–19, 23.

38. See *Declaration of Conscience: An Appeal to South Africa,* cosponsored by Eleanor Roosevelt, Bishop James A. Pike, and Martin Luther King Jr., and drafted and promoted by the American Committee on Africa, New York (July 1957), King Center Library and Archives, 1–2; Lewis V. Baldwin, *Toward the Beloved Community: Martin Luther King, Jr., and South Africa* (Cleveland: Pilgrim, 1995), 16; and Martin Luther King Jr. to Rabbi Seymour J. Cohen (September 8, 1965), King Center Library and Archives, 1.

39. This claim is supported by a careful examination of King's movement prayers. See Baldwin, ed., *Never Alone,* 43–59. For King's views on the subject, see King, *Strength to Love,* 131–33; and Bowyer et al., *Prayer in the Black Tradition,* 64–65.

40. Carson et al., eds., *Papers of Martin Luther King, Jr.,* 6:590–91; King, *Strength to Love,* 131–33; King, *The Trumpet Of Conscience,* 59; Bowyer et al., *Prayer in the Black Tradition,* 64–65; and Mervyn A. Warren, *King Came Preaching: The Pulpit Power of Dr. Martin Luther King Jr.* (Downers Grove, Ill.: InterVarsity, 2001), 40–41, 136, 158.

41. Baldwin, *To Make the Wounded Whole,* 294; Baldwin, *Toward the Beloved Community,* 65–185; and Baldwin et al., *The Legacy of Martin Luther King, Jr.,* 36–51, 101–9, 154–58, 253–89.

42. King, *Strength to Love,* 131–32; Washington, ed., *A Testament of Hope,* 84; King, *Stride toward Freedom,* 63, 134–35; and Carson and Holloran, eds., *A Knock at Midnight,* 160–63.

43. DeWolf, "Funeral Tribute to Martin Luther King, Jr.," 1.

INDEX